OPPOSING
VIEWPOINTS®
SERIES

| Water

Other Books of Related Interest:

Opposing Viewpoints Series

Global Warming

Globalization

Health

The North and South Poles

The United Nations

Current Controversies Series

Aid to Africa

Conserving the Environment

The Global Food Crisis

At Issue Series

Adaptation and Climate Change

Greenhouse Gases

"Congress shall make no law . . . abridging the freedom of speech, or of the press."

First Amendment to the U.S. Constitution

The basic foundation of our democracy is the First Amendment guarantee of freedom of expression. The Opposing Viewpoints Series is dedicated to the concept of this basic freedom and the idea that it is more important to practice it than to enshrine it.

OPPOSING
VIEWPOINTS®
SERIES

| Water

Jacqueline Langwith, Book Editor

GREENHAVEN PRESS
A part of Gale, Cengage Learning

GALE
CENGAGE Learning™

Detroit • New York • San Francisco • New Haven, Conn • Waterville, Maine • London

GALE
CENGAGE Learning

Christine Nasso, *Publisher*
Elizabeth Des Chenes, *Managing Editor*

© 2010 Greenhaven Press, a part of Gale, Cengage Learning.

Gale and Greenhaven Press are registered trademarks used herein under license.

For more information, contact:
Greenhaven Press
27500 Drake Rd.
Farmington Hills, MI 48331-3535
Or you can visit our Internet site at gale.cengage.com

For product information and technology assistance, contact us at

Gale Customer Support, 1-800-877-4253
For permission to use material from this text or product, submit all requests online at www.cengage.com/permissions

Further permissions questions can be emailed to permissionrequest@cengage.com

Articles in Greenhaven Press anthologies are often edited for length to meet page requirements. In addition, original titles of these works are changed to clearly present the main thesis and to explicitly indicate the author's opinion. Every effort is made to ensure that Greenhaven Press accurately reflects the original intent of the authors. Every effort has been made to trace the owners of copyrighted material.

Cover photographs © Photodisc/Getty Images and Anatole Branch/Digital Vision/Getty Images.

LIBRARY OF CONGRESS CATALOGING-IN-PUBLICATION DATA

Water / Jacqueline Langwith, book editor.
    p. cm. -- (Opposing viewpoints)
    Includes bibliographical references and index.
    978-0-7377-4546-7 (hardcover)
    978-0-7377-4547-4 (pbk.)
    1. Water-supply. 2. Water resources development. 3. Water quality. I. Langwith, Jacqueline.
    TD348.W377 2009
    363.6'1--dc22
                                                        2009022929

Printed in the United States of America
1 2 3 4 5 6 7 13 12 11 10 09

Contents

Chapter 3: How Should Water Resources Be Managed?

Chapter 4: Is Drinking Water Safe?

Why Consider Opposing Viewpoints?

> *"The only way in which a human being can make some approach to knowing the whole of a subject is by hearing what can be said about it by persons of every variety of opinion and studying all modes in which it can be looked at by every character of mind. No wise man ever acquired his wisdom in any mode but this."*
>
> John Stuart Mill

In our media-intensive culture it is not difficult to find differing opinions. Thousands of newspapers and magazines and dozens of radio and television talk shows resound with differing points of view. The difficulty lies in deciding which opinion to agree with and which "experts" seem the most credible. The more inundated we become with differing opinions and claims, the more essential it is to hone critical reading and thinking skills to evaluate these ideas. Opposing Viewpoints books address this problem directly by presenting stimulating debates that can be used to enhance and teach these skills. The varied opinions contained in each book examine many different aspects of a single issue. While examining these conveniently edited opposing views, readers can develop critical thinking skills such as the ability to compare and contrast authors' credibility, facts, argumentation styles, use of persuasive techniques, and other stylistic tools. In short, the Opposing Viewpoints Series is an ideal way to attain the higher-level thinking and reading skills so essential in a culture of diverse and contradictory opinions.

In addition to providing a tool for critical thinking, Opposing Viewpoints books challenge readers to question their own strongly held opinions and assumptions. Most people form their opinions on the basis of upbringing, peer pressure, and personal, cultural, or professional bias. By reading carefully balanced opposing views, readers must directly confront new ideas as well as the opinions of those with whom they disagree. This is not to simplistically argue that everyone who reads opposing views will—or should—change his or her opinion. Instead, the series enhances readers' understanding of their own views by encouraging confrontation with opposing ideas. Careful examination of others' views can lead to the readers' understanding of the logical inconsistencies in their own opinions, perspective on why they hold an opinion, and the consideration of the possibility that their opinion requires further evaluation.

Evaluating Other Opinions

To ensure that this type of examination occurs, Opposing Viewpoints books present all types of opinions. Prominent spokespeople on different sides of each issue as well as well-known professionals from many disciplines challenge the reader. An additional goal of the series is to provide a forum for other, less known, or even unpopular viewpoints. The opinion of an ordinary person who has had to make the decision to cut off life support from a terminally ill relative, for example, may be just as valuable and provide just as much insight as a medical ethicist's professional opinion. The editors have two additional purposes in including these less known views. One, the editors encourage readers to respect others' opinions—even when not enhanced by professional credibility. It is only by reading or listening to and objectively evaluating others' ideas that one can determine whether they are worthy of consideration. Two, the inclusion of such viewpoints encourages the important critical thinking skill of objectively evaluating an author's credentials and bias. This evaluation will illuminate an author's reasons for taking a particular stance on an issue and will aid in readers' evaluation of the author's ideas.

It is our hope that these books will give readers a deeper understanding of the issues debated and an appreciation of the complexity of even seemingly simple issues when good and honest people disagree. This awareness is particularly important in a democratic society such as ours in which people enter into public debate to determine the common good. Those with whom one disagrees should not be regarded as enemies but rather as people whose views deserve careful examination and may shed light on one's own.

Thomas Jefferson once said that "difference of opinion leads to inquiry, and inquiry to truth." Jefferson, a broadly educated man, argued that "if a nation expects to be ignorant and free . . . it expects what never was and never will be." As individuals and as a nation, it is imperative that we consider the opinions of others and examine them with skill and discernment. The Opposing Viewpoints Series is intended to help readers achieve this goal.

David L. Bender and Bruno Leone,
Founders

Introduction

In January 2004, *Opportunity* and *Spirit* landed on Mars to begin their mission—find evidence that Mars can or ever did support life. The twin rovers were equipped with cameras, microscopes, and several spectrometers to analyze rocks and soils. Their goal was to find geological clues about whether water was ever present on Mars. Water is essential for life as we know it. So, *Opportunity*'s and *Spirit*'s missions were not surprising. *Opportunity* quickly found evidence that a large body of salty water may have been present on Mars. Later, *Spirit* found that water may have existed in the cracks of some volcanic rocks. On March 19, 2009, the National Aeronautics and Space Administration (NASA) reported that *Opportunity* and *Spirit* were still roaming around Mars collecting data, more than five years after their mission began. As *Opportunity* and *Spirit* gather evidence about water on Mars, scientists here on Earth debate the origin of water on our planet. Two dominant theories suggest how earthly water arose: the "inside-out" model proposes that water was present when Earth formed—attached to minerals in the mantle—and pushed to the surface through volcanic eruptions; the "outside-in" theory proposes that Earth's water came from comets or asteroids that bombarded Earth's surface billions of years ago.

Water has so many unique properties, it is no wonder why it is essential for life. Water is the only natural substance that is found in all three states—liquid, solid (ice), and gas (steam)—at the temperatures normally found on Earth. Additionally, it is one of the few substances of which the solid form is less dense than the liquid form—this is why ice floats on top of water. This property is critical for Earth's ecosystems. If ice was denser than liquid water, the lakes and oceans in cold climates would freeze solid, killing the fish and creatures within them. Water's high surface tension makes it sticky and elastic, and causes it to clump together in drops. Water's surface tension is also responsible for capillary action, which allows water to move through the roots of plants and through the tiny blood vessels in our bodies. Anywhere from 55 percent to 78 percent of the human body is composed of water. All of the metabolic processes that occur in our bodies, from the breakdown of food to the beating of our hearts, are enabled by water. It seems an understatement to say that water enabled life to form on planet Earth.

Because of Earth's relatively close distance to the sun, researchers do not believe that liquid water was present on Earth's surface when it formed about 4.5 billion years ago. Earth's surface was blisteringly hot then, and water would have bubbled up and evaporated away instantly. A few hundred million years later, however, Earth became sufficiently cool and hospitable to water. Scientists are pretty certain that by about 3.9 to 4.2 billion years ago, liquid water was present on Earth's surface. But where did the water, which covers 70 percent of Earth's surface, come from? Proponents of the inside-out model believe that the water in our oceans came from within Earth. This theory is based on the absorption of water by the minerals and dust that formed Earth. According to research performed by University of Arizona Professor Michael Drake, many common minerals can absorb astonishing amounts of water. Drake thinks the minerals, which along with a swirling cloud of dust and gases, coalesced to form Earth could easily have absorbed enough water to fill the oceans nearly ten times over. Volcanic eruptions would have released the water from the minerals and spewed it to Earth's surface as steam. When Earth's surface was cool enough, the steam would have condensed to form the first earthly oceans. Drake is confident that Earth's water came from within. He says, "For me it's a no-brainer. At least some, if not most, of Earth's water had to come from adsorption of water onto grains before the planet ever formed."

Despite Drake's confidence in the inside-out theory, many other scientists believe that Earth's water originally came from outer space. The outside-in theory proposes that most of Earth's water came from icy comets or asteroids, which bombarded young Earth for hundreds of millions of years. Comets seem like a good bet to be the origin of Earth's water. Described as "dirty snow balls" by famous astronomer Fred Whipple, comets are known to consist mainly of ice. In 1999, however, scientists from California Technological University analyzed emissions coming from the comet Hale-Bopp and found that the level of deuterium, an isotope of hydrogen, in the comet did not match the level of deuterium in Earth's oceans. If comets gave Earth its water supply billions of years ago, then the oceans should have roughly the same amount of deuterium as comets. To some the isotope discrepancy provided doubt that the outside-in theory was correct.

Some of the doubt about the outside-in theory was erased in 2006, however, with the discovery of large, asteroid-like comets from a region of space known as the main belt. The main belt comets, as they are called, are very much like asteroids—rocky and large—but also like comets in that they contain significant amounts of ice. Some scientists think it is likely that the isotope levels in these asteroid-like comets matches the isotope level in Earth's oceans. Thus, they believe the main belt comets are the source of Earth's water. According to Professor David Jewitt from the University of Hawaii, discoverer of the main belt comets, these comets "may illuminate the sources of the terrestrial planet volatiles (e.g., water), including the origin of the Earth's oceans. If Earth formed hot, consistent with its large size and gravitational potential, then water and other volatiles might have been added later, after the surface had cooled down. The outer asteroid belt—home of the main belt comets—is a leading candidate source region for this so-called 'late veneer' of added volatiles."

Some scientists think both the inside-out and the outside-in theories may be correct. Kathrin Altwegg, a comet expert from Bern University in Switzerland, thinks some of Earth's water may have come from comets and some from within Earth. To know for sure, more research is needed, contends Altwegg. She thinks that determining the isotope ratio in the main belt comets and in other planets in our solar system, such as Mars, will help clarify the source of earthly water. These answers may come soon as NASA has sent another "rover," the *Phoenix Mars Lander*, to Mars. One of the most important missions of the *Mars Lander* is to measure the deuterium-to-hydrogen ratio in Martian water. Says Altwegg, "It will be really interesting once we analyze water on Mars, and it would be funny if Mars did not get water in the same way as the earth."

Wherever Earth's water came from billions of years ago, it is still here today. Water cycles between Earth and the atmosphere, but it never leaves. In addition to differing opinions about the origin of Earth's water, scientists, policy makers, concerned citizens, and environmental and humanitarian organizations have differing opinions on many other water related issues. In *Opposing Viewpoints: Water*, the contributors provide their thoughts about water-related issues, in the following chapters: "What Are the Major Issues Affecting Water Resources?" "Is There a Water Crisis?" "How Should Water Resources Be Managed?" and "Is Drinking Water Safe?"

CHAPTER 1

What Are the Major Issues Affecting Water Resources?

Chapter Preface

Nearly three-quarters of Earth is made up of oceans. These vast waters have always been important to mankind for travel and food. Since the dawn of the industrial age, oceans have also been a source of energy reserves. The continental shelf, the gently sloping landmass that extends out from under the North American continent until it meets the open ocean, is a rich source of fossil fuels. About 25 percent of domestically produced oil and natural gas are derived from continental shelf reserves located off the coasts of California, Alaska, and the western Gulf of Mexico. Other offshore reserves around the United States, however, are not producing oil or gas. They have generally been off limits to drilling. Some Americans think these untapped offshore oil and gas reserves should be opened up because they are critical for U.S. energy independence. Others think that the environmental risks of drilling in the ocean are too great, however, and that these offshore reserves should remain off limits.

Offshore drilling is allowed in some federally controlled areas of the ocean. Individual states control offshore drilling up to three miles away from their coastal shores. The federal government controls offshore drilling beyond three miles and up to about two hundred miles from the coast, a region known as the outer continental shelf. Drilling has been allowed for quite some time in both state and federal waters off the coasts of Texas, Louisiana, and Alabama. This area—namely, the western Gulf of Mexico—is one of the major offshore oil and gas producing areas in the country. Additionally, as of April 2009, there were dozens of drilling platforms in federal waters off the coast of Alaska and in some limited areas off the California coast.

In 2008, long-standing federal policies, which placed many coastal areas off limits to drilling, were allowed to lapse or were eliminated. In June 1990, President George H.W. Bush issued an executive directive ordering the Department of Interior not to allow offshore drilling in coastal areas other than Texas, Louisiana, Alabama, and limited parts of Alaska. President Bill Clinton extended this moratorium until June 2012. The moratorium affected virtually all of the coasts of the North Atlantic, California, Washington, Oregon, New England, the Mid-Atlantic, and the Northern Aleutian Basin. It also included the eastern Gulf of Mexico off the coast of southwestern Florida. Bush's directive expanded a moratorium Congress imposed in 1982 that removed 736,000 acres off the coast of northern and central California from leasing for oil and gas exploration and production. In June 2008, President George W. Bush lifted the moratorium first established by his father and extended by President Clinton. Then in October 2008, U.S. Congress allowed the congressional moratorium to lapse.

Many Americans think offshore drilling should be allowed in these previously off-limits areas. During the 2008 presidential election, Republican candidate John McCain and his running mate, Sarah Palin, expressed support for expanded offshore drilling. At the Republican National Convention in August 2008, Palin said, "We Americans need to produce more of our own oil and gas, and take it from a gal who knows the North Slope of Alaska: we've got lots of both." She continued: "Our opponents say, again and again, that drilling will not solve all of America's energy problems—as if we all didn't know that already. But the fact that drilling won't solve every problem is no excuse to do nothing at all."

Organizations such as the Heritage Foundation, the Cato Institute, and the Pacific Research Institute also support more offshore drilling. They contend that vast amounts of oil and natural gas reserves are estimated to lie beneath these restricted areas. In an April 13, 2009, *Newsweek* article calling for a change in energy policy—including more offshore drilling—Republican Newt Gingrich asserted that there "are 86 billion barrels of oil and 420 trillion cubic feet of natural gas lying undeveloped offshore." Proponents of drilling contend that these reserves should be tapped to help increase supplies, reduce reliance on foreign oil, and lower prices at the pump. Additionally, they say, the environmental risks of offshore drilling have been minimized. According to Ben Lieberman from the Heritage Foundation, "OCS [outer continental shelf] restrictions are a relic of the past. They were put in place at a time when energy was cheap, the need for additional domestic supplies was not seen as dire, and the political path of least resistance was to give in to environmentalists. All that has changed, with more than a quadrupling of oil and natural gas prices since the restrictions were first imposed. Extra energy is badly needed, and the risk of producing it has been reduced." Palin, Gingrich, Lieberman, and many other people believe it would be wise for the United States to expand offshore drilling.

On the other side of the debate are national and state environmental organizations. They contend that oil and gas drilling in the oceans is simply too environmentally risky and the rewards too small. According to the organization Environment Florida, "At each stage of testing, exploration, and production, the oil and gas business produces contaminated water, uses toxic drilling muds, and periodically spills oil and toxic liquids into the ocean. Pollutants like mercury and persistent hydrocarbons contaminate fish and sea life near platforms and massive spills kill seabirds, sea turtles, fish, and marine mammals." In addition to opposing drilling because of its environmental risks, Environment Florida and other organizations do not think the country can drill its way out of lower gas prices or create energy independence. According to Greenpeace USA, "The United States burns 24 percent of the world's oil, yet we only have 3 percent of the world's oil reserves. Even if we drilled every drop of oil the U.S. has on shore or off its coasts, we will never be able to drill our way to lower oil prices or energy security." Greenpeace also contends that it will be years before offshore oil exploration could begin and years after that before production would start. "If any effect were to be felt on gas prices (most likely only a few pennies per gallon), that effect is decades away. Offering up more of our coastline for drilling won't lower gas prices," says Greenpeace. Organizations like Environment Florida and Greenpeace USA think offshore drilling is a bad idea.

The debate about offshore oil and gas drilling does not appear to be going away any time soon. Proponents of drilling are worried that President Barack Obama will reinstate the moratorium on federal drilling, which was lifted by President George W. Bush. Opponents of drilling are worried that he won't reverse it, however, and that drilling will eventually occur in some pristine offshore areas. Like the offshore drilling debate, discussions centered on the world's water—its oceans, lakes, rivers, streams, and underground aquifers—occur every day in regions all over the world. In the following chapter, the contributors provide their opinions on some of the major issues affecting the world's water resources.

| "*Business-as-usual global warming would almost surely send the planet beyond a tipping point, guaranteeing a disastrous degree of sea level rise.*"

Global Warming Threatens Massive Sea Level Rise

James Hansen

In the following viewpoint, James Hansen contends that massive sea level rise brought about by global warming is a near certainty unless something is done to curtail greenhouse gases. A majority of scientists believe that atmospheric increases in greenhouse gases, particularly carbon dioxide, are causing the earth to warm. Scientists aren't entirely certain of the future impacts of a warmed earth. Evidence indicates that the levels of oceans and seas around the world will rise, but scientists don't agree on the extent of the rise. Hansen is convinced that a global temperature increase of two to three degrees Celsius—what he calls a business-as-usual global warming scenario—will cause ice sheets in Antarctica or Greenland to melt in a rapid, nonlinear fashion and this will cause massive sea level rise. Hansen explains why he believes ice sheets can melt so rapidly and why he thinks such

James Hansen, "Huge Sea Level Rises Are Coming—Unless We Act Now," *New Scientist*, July 25, 2007. Copyright © 2007 Reed Elsevier Business Publishing, Ltd. Reproduced by permission. www.newscientist.com.

rapid ice melts will cause a disastrous rise in sea levels. Hansen is puzzled as to why more scientists don't speak out about the risks of sea level changes and call for more restrictions on greenhouse gas emissions. James Hansen is a physicist, an astronomer, and the head of NASA's Goddard Institute for Space Studies in New York. He has spoken about climate change since the 1980s.

As you read, consider the following questions:

1. According to Hansen, oxygen isotopes in deep-ocean fossil plankton reveal that the last time the earth was two to three degrees Celsius warmer was around 3 million years ago. What are these deep-ocean fossil plankton known as?

2. According to Hansen, what is the Intergovernmental Panel on Climate Change's (IPCC's) latest projection for sea level rise this century?

3. Hansen says the threat of sea level change is the reason he is calling for the global community to restrict global warming to less than one degree Celsius above the 2000 temperature. This would imply a carbon dioxide (CO_2) limit of about what, according to Hansen?

I find it almost inconceivable that "business as usual" climate change will not result in a rise in sea level measured in metres within a century. Am I the only scientist who thinks so?

Last year I testified in a case brought by car manufacturers to challenge California's new laws on vehicle emissions. Under questioning from the lawyer, I conceded that I was not a glaciologist. The lawyer then asked me to identify glaciologists who agreed publicly with my assertion that sea level is likely to rise more than a metre this century if greenhouse gas emissions continue to grow: "Name one!"

I could not, at that moment. I was dismayed, because in conversations and e-mail exchanges with relevant scientists I sensed a deep concern about the stability of ice sheets in the face of "business as usual" global warming scenarios, which assume that emissions of greenhouse gases will continue to increase. Why might scientists be reticent to express concerns about something so important?

Pressure on Scientists

I suspect it is because of what I call the "John Mercer effect". In 1978, when global warming was beginning to get attention from government agencies, Mercer suggested that global warming could lead to disastrous disintegration of the West Antarctic ice sheet. Although it was not obvious who was right on the science, I noticed that researchers who suggested that his paper was alarmist were regarded as more authoritative.

It seems to me that scientists downplaying the dangers of climate change fare better when it comes to getting funding. Drawing attention to the dangers of global warming may or may not have helped increase funding for the relevant scientific areas, but it surely did not help individuals like Mercer who stuck their heads out.

I can vouch for that from my own experience. After I published a paper in 1981 that described the likely effects of fossil fuel use, the US Department of Energy reversed a decision to fund my group's research, specifically criticising aspects of that paper.

I believe there is pressure on scientists to be conservative. Caveats are essential to science. They are born in scepticism, and scepticism is at the heart of the scientific method and discovery. However, in a case such as ice sheet instability and sea level rise, excessive caution also holds dangers. "Scientific reticence" can hinder communication with the public about the dangers of global warming. We may rue reticence if it means no action is taken until it is too late to prevent future disasters.

Wet Process

So why do I think a sea level rise of metres would be a near certainty if greenhouse gas emissions keep increasing? Because while the growth of great ice sheets takes millennia, the disintegration of ice sheets is a wet process that can proceed rapidly.

Sea level is already rising at a moderate rate. In the past decade, it increased by 3 centimetres, about double the average rate during the preceding century. The rate of sea level rise over the 20th century was itself probably greater than the rate in the prior millennium, and this is due at least in part to human activity. About half of the increase is accounted for by thermal expansion of ocean water as a result of global warming. Melting mountain glaciers worldwide are responsible for several centimetres of the increase.

Greenland and Antarctica are also contributing to the rise in recent years. Gravity measurements by the GRACE [Gravity Recovery and Climate Experiment] satellites have recently shown that the ice sheets of Greenland and West Antarctica are each losing about 150 cubic kilometres of ice per year. Spread over the oceans, this is close to 1 millimetre a year, or 10 centimetres per century.

Runaway Ice Sheet Collapse

The current rate of sea level change is not without consequences. However, the primary issue is whether global warming will reach a level such that ice sheets begin to disintegrate in a rapid, non-linear fashion on West Antarctica, Greenland or both. Once well under way, such a collapse might be impossible to stop, because there are multiple positive feedbacks. In that event, a sea level rise of several metres at least would be expected.

As an example, let us say that ice sheet melting adds 1 centimetre to sea level for the decade 2005 to 2015, and that this doubles each decade until the West Antarctic ice sheet is largely depleted. This would yield a rise in sea level of more than 5 metres by 2095.

Of course, I cannot prove that my choice of a 10-year doubling time is accurate but I'd bet $1000 to a doughnut that it provides a far better estimate of the ice sheet's contribution to sea level rise than a linear response. In my opinion, if the world warms by 2 °C to 3 °C, such massive sea level rise is inevitable, and a substantial fraction of the rise would occur within a century. Business-as-usual global warming would almost surely send the planet beyond a tipping point, guaranteeing a disastrous degree of sea level rise.

Although some ice sheet experts believe that the ice sheets are more stable, I believe that their view is partly based on the faulty assumption that the earth has been as much as 2 °C warmer in previous interglacial periods, when the sea level was at most a few metres higher than at present. There is strong evidence that the earth now is within 1 °C of its highest temperature in the past million years. Oxygen isotopes in the deep-ocean fossil plankton known as foraminifera reveal that the earth was last 2 °C to 3 °C warmer around 3 million years ago, with carbon dioxide levels of perhaps 350 to 450 parts per million. It was a dramatically different planet then, with no Arctic sea ice in the warm seasons and sea level about 25 metres higher, give or take 10 metres.

Models Are Underestimating Global Warming and Sea Level Rise

There is not a sufficiently widespread appreciation of the implications of putting back into the air a large fraction of the carbon stored in the ground over epochs of geologic time. The climate forcing caused by these greenhouse gases would dwarf the climate forcing for any time in the past several hundred thousand years—the period for which accurate records of atmospheric composition are available from ice cores.

Models based on the business-as-usual scenarios of the Intergovernmental Panel on Climate Change (IPCC) predict a global warming of at least 3 °C by the end of this century. What many people do not realise is that these models generally include only fast feedback processes: changes in sea ice, clouds, water vapour and aerosols. Actual global warming would be greater as slow feedbacks come into play: increased vegetation at high latitudes, ice sheet shrinkage and further greenhouse gas emissions from the land and sea in response to global warming.

The IPCC's latest projection for sea level rise this century is 18 to 59 centimetres. Though it explicitly notes that it was unable to include possible dynamical responses of the ice sheets in its calculations, the provision of such specific numbers encourages a predictable public belief that the projected sea level change is moderate, and indeed smaller than in the previous IPCC report. There have been numerous media reports of "reduced" predictions of sea level rise, and commentators have denigrated suggestions that business-as-usual emissions may cause a sea level rise measured in metres. However, if these IPCC numbers are taken as predictions of actual sea level rise, as they have been by the public, they imply that the ice sheets can miraculously survive a business-as-usual climate forcing assault for a millennium or longer.

There are glaciologists who anticipate such long response times, because their ice sheet models have been designed to match past climate changes. However, work by my group shows that the typical 6000-year timescale for ice sheet disintegration in the past reflects the gradual changes in Earth's orbit that drove climate changes at the time, rather than any inherent limit for how long it takes ice sheets to disintegrate.

Growing Evidence of Massive Sea Level Rise

Indeed, the palaeoclimate record contains numerous examples of ice sheets yielding sea level rises of several metres per century when forcings were smaller than that of the business-as-usual scenario. For example, about 14,000 years ago, sea level rose approximately 20 metres in 400 years, or about 1 metre every 20 years.

There is growing evidence that the global warming already under way could bring a comparably rapid rise in sea level. The process begins with human-made greenhouse gases, which cause the atmosphere to be more opaque to infrared radiation, thus decreasing radiation of heat to space. As a result, the earth is gaining more heat than it is losing: currently 0.5 to 1 watts per square metre. This planetary energy imbalance is sufficient to melt ice corresponding to 1 metre of sea level rise per decade, if the extra energy were used entirely for that purpose—and the energy imbalance could double if emissions keep growing.

So where is the extra energy going? A small part of it is warming the atmosphere and thus contributing to one key feedback on the ice sheets: the "albedo flip" that occurs when snow and ice begin to melt. Snow-covered ice reflects back to space most of the sunlight striking it, but as warming air causes melting on the surface, the darker ice absorbs much more solar energy. This increases the planetary energy imbalance and can lead to more melting. Most of the resulting meltwater burrows through the ice sheet, lubricating its base and speeding up the discharge of icebergs to the ocean.

The area with summer melt on Greenland has increased from around 450,000 square kilometres when satellite observations began in 1979 to more than 600,000 square kilometres in 2002. Seismometers around the world have detected an increasing number of earthquakes on Greenland near the outlets of major ice streams. The earthquakes are an indication that large pieces of the ice sheet lurch forward and then grind to a halt because of friction with the ground. The number of these "ice quakes" doubled between 1993 and the late 1990s, and it has since doubled again. It is not yet clear whether the quake

Sea Level Rise Is Greatest Global Warming Risk

The ice sheets on Greenland and West Antarctica store enough water to raise global sea level by about 40 feet if completely released to the ocean. Scientists do not believe that a complete release could happen instantaneously, but even a small portion of this ice released over the span of several decades would generate extreme impacts from SLR [sea level rise] for millions of people. Because of this fact and the surprising dynamical changes observed in these ice sheets recently, their potential collapse may be the greatest long-term risk humans face from global warming, although there are many serious near-term risks as well, such as more extreme weather events, decreased water supplies, and disruption of many natural ecosystems.

Pew Center on Global Climate Change,
"Sea Level Rise—The State of the Science,"
February 2, 2007. www.pewclimate.org.

number is proportional to ice loss, but the rapid increase is cause for concern about the long-term stability of the ice sheet.

Summer Melt

Additional global warming of 2 °C to 3 °C is expected to cause local warming of about 5 °C over Greenland. This would spread summer melt over practically the entire ice sheet and considerably lengthen the melt season. In my opinion it is inconceivable that the ice sheet could withstand such increased meltwater for long before starting to disintegrate rapidly, but it is very difficult to predict when such a period of large, rapid change would begin.

Summer melt on West Antarctica has received less attention than on Greenland, but it is more important. The West Antarctic ice sheet, which rests on bedrock far below sea level, is more vulnerable as it is being attacked from below by warming ocean water, as well as from above by a warming atmosphere. Satellite observations reveal increasing areas of summer melt on the West Antarctic ice sheet, and also a longer melt season.

The warming atmosphere and increased absorption of sunlight are not the only factors that will increase surface melt. If there is a significant loss of ice, the surfaces of the ice sheets will be at lower altitudes, where the air is warmer, causing additional melt: another positive feedback.

Most of the excess energy due to the planetary imbalance is going into the ocean rather than the atmosphere, because it takes about 1000 times as much energy to heat the oceans by 1 °C as it does to heat the atmosphere as much. The acceleration of ice sheet disintegration depends on how much of the extra ocean heat is transferred to the ice.

Accelerating Glaciers

This transfer can occur in two main ways: by the speeding up of glaciers resulting in more ice being discharged into the oceans, and by direct transfer of heat from the water underneath and against fringing ice shelves. Since fringing ice shelves float on water, their melting does not raise sea level directly. However, ice shelves hold back the ice sheets resting on land or on the seabed, so as the ice shelves melt or break up, the ice streams draining the ice sheets accelerate, providing another positive feedback effect.

An example was recently seen on the Antarctic Peninsula. The combined effect of surface melt and ice shelf thinning from below led to the sudden collapse of the Larsen B ice shelf, which was followed by the acceleration of glacial tributaries far inland.

Positive feedback from loss of buttressing ice shelves will influence some Greenland ice streams, but the West Antarctic ice sheet will be affected much more. The local warming and melt that preceded the Larsen B collapse was only a fraction of the expected warming in the West Antarctic under business-as-usual scenarios. In fact, observations show the ocean around West Antarctica is already warming, ice shelves are thinning by several metres per year, and glaciers are discharging more icebergs.

There are also some negative feedbacks, in the short term at least. As the discharge of ice increases, regional cooling by the icebergs will be significant. This cooling can lead to increased sea ice and cloud cover, and thus increased reflection of sunlight. However, cooling of the ocean surface by melting ice also reduces heat radiation from the water surface. This increases the planetary energy imbalance, thus supplying additional energy for ice melt. Models confirm that the cooling effect of melting ice is temporary and that there will be a net increase in ocean heat uptake around West Antarctica and Greenland as greenhouse gases increase.

Higher Snowfall

Another negative feedback is increasing snowfall on ice sheet interiors, because of the higher moisture content of the warming atmosphere. Some models predict that ice sheets will grow overall with global warming, but those models do not include realistic processes of ice sheet disintegration. Palaeoclimate data confirms the common-sense expectation that the net effect is for ice sheets to shrink as the world warms, as the GRACE satellites show is happening already.

The findings in the Antarctic are the most disconcerting. Warming there has been limited in recent decades, in part due to the effects of ozone depletion. The fact that West Antarctica is losing mass at a significant rate suggests that the thinning ice shelves are already beginning to affect ice discharge rates.

So far, warming of the ocean surface around Antarctica has been small compared with the rest of the world, as models predict, but that limited warming is expected to increase. The detection of recent, increasing summer surface melt on West Antarctica raises the danger that feedbacks among these processes could lead to non-linear growth of ice discharge from Antarctica.

This problem is urgent. The non-linear response could easily run out of control, both because of the positive feedbacks and because of inertias in the system.

Scientists Should Speak Out, Massive Sea Level Rise a Near Certainty

Ocean warming and thus melting of ice shelves will continue even if CO_2 levels are stabilised, because the ocean response time is long and the temperature at depth is far from equilibrium for current forcing. Ice sheets also have inertia and are far from equilibrium. There is also inertia in human systems: even if it is decided that changes must be made, it may take decades to replace infrastructure.

The threat of large sea level change is a principal element in my argument that the global community must aim to restrict any further global warming to less than 1 °C above the temperature in 2000. This implies a CO_2 limit of about 450 parts per million or less. Such scenarios require almost immediate changes to get energy and greenhouse gas emissions onto a fundamentally different path.

Is my perspective on this problem really so different than that of other relevant members of the scientific community? Based on interactions with others, I conclude that there is not such a great gap. The apparent differences may arise partly from a natural reluctance to speak out.

Reticence is fine for the IPCC. Individual scientists also can choose to stay within a comfort zone, and not worry that they may say something that proves to be slightly wrong. But perhaps we should consider our legacy from a broader perspective. Do we not know enough to say more? Using the fact that a glacier on Greenland slowed after speeding up as "proof" that reticence is appropriate is little different from the common misconception that a cold weather snap disproves global warming.

The broader picture strongly indicates that ice sheets will respond in a non-linear fashion to global warming—and are already beginning to do so. There is enough information now, in my opinion, to make it a near certainty that business-as-usual scenarios will lead to disastrous multi-metre sea level rise on the century time scale.

| "All this talk that sea level is rising, this stems from the computer modeling, not from observations. The observations don't find it!"

Sea Levels Will Not Rise Because of Global Warming

Nils-Axel Mörner, as told to Gregory Murphy

In the following viewpoint, Gregory Murphy of LaRouche's Executive Intelligence Review interviews sea level specialist Nils-Axel Mörner. Mörner contends that sea levels are not rising at all and that one hundred years from now they will be only slightly higher than they are now—regardless of how much carbon dioxide is pumped into the air. Mörner bases his assertion that sea levels are not rising on observational data, not computer modeling, which he says is the only evidence for sea level rise. He says that observational data from the last three hundred years shows that sea levels have gone up and down with absolutely no rising trend. He believes that global warming and sea level rise are stories perpetuated by the Intergovernmental Panel on Climate Change and are supported by those who would stand to gain from its acceptance, such as small island nations and

Nils-Axel Mörner, as told to Gregory Murphy, "Claim That Sea Level Is Rising Is a Total Fraud," *Executive Intelligence Review*, June 22, 2007, pp. 33–37. Copyright © 2007 EIRNS. All rights reserved. Reproduced by permission. www.climatechangefacts.info.

global warming researchers. The Executive Intelligence Review *is a publication of Lyndon LaRouche, a controversial political and cultural figure. Mörner retired as head of the Paleogeophysics and Geodynamics Department at Stockholm University in 2005.*

As you read, consider the following questions:

1. Mörner says he was exceptionally surprised by the number of sea level specialists who were authors for the Intergovernmental Panel on Climate Change (IPCC). According to Mörner, how many of the twenty-two IPCC authors were sea level specialists?

2. According to Mörner, why is the glacier Kilimanjaro melting?

3. What is Mörner's improved (by considering that we're going into a cold phase) prediction of how much sea levels will rise in one hundred years?

*(E*IR) [Executive Intelligence Review]: *I would like to start with a little bit about your background, and some of the commissions and research groups you've worked on.*

Dr. Nils-Axel Mörner: I am a sea-level specialist. There are many good sea-level people in the world, but let's put it this way: There's no one who's beaten me. I took my thesis in 1969, devoted to a large extent to the sea-level problem. From then on, I have launched most of the new theories, in the '70s, '80s, and '90s. I was the one who understood the problem of the gravitational potential surface, the theory that it changes with time. I'm the one who studied the rotation of the earth, how it affected the redistribution of the oceans' masses. And so on. And then I was president of INQUA [International Union for Quaternary Research], an international fraternal association, their Commission on Sea-Level Changes and Coastal Evolution, from 1999 to 2003. And in order to do something intelligent there, we launched a special international sea-level research project in the Maldives, because that's the hottest spot on Earth for—there are so many variables interacting there, so it was interesting, and also people had claimed that the Maldives—about 1,200 small islands—were doomed to disappear in 50 years, or at most, 100 years. So that was a very important target.

Then I have had my own research institute at Stockholm University, which was devoted to something called paleogeophysics and geodynamics. . . .

The last ten years or so, of course, everything has been the discussion on sea level, which they say is drowning us; in the early '90s, I was in Washington giving a paper on how the sea level is *not* rising, as they said. That had some echoes around the world.

What is the real state of the sea-level rising?

You have to look at that in a lot of different ways. That is what I have done in a lot of different papers, so we can confine ourselves to the short story here. One way is to look at the global picture, to try to find the essence of what is going on. And then we can see that the sea level was indeed rising, from, let us say, 1850 to 1930–40. And that rise had a rate in the order of 1 millimeter per year. Not more. 1.1 is the exact figure. And we can check that, because Holland is a subsiding area; it has been subsiding for many millions of years; and Sweden, after the last Ice Age, was uplifted. So if you balance those, there is only one solution, and it will be this figure.

That ended in 1940, and there had been no rise until 1970; and then we can come into the debate here on what is going on, and we have to go to satellite altimetry, and I will return to that. But before doing that: There's another way of checking it, because if the radius of the earth increases, because sea level is rising, then immediately the earth's rate of rotation would slow down. That is a physical law, right? You have it in figure-skating: when they rotate very fast, the arms are close to the body; and then when they increase the radius, by putting out their arms, they stop by themselves. So you can look at the rotation and the same comes up: Yes, it might be 1.1 mm per year, but absolutely not more. It could be less, because there could be other factors affecting the Earth, but it certainly could not be more. Absolutely not! Again, it's a matter of physics.

So, we have this 1 mm per year up to 1930, by observation, and we have it by rotation recording. So we go with those two. They go up and down, but there's no trend in it; it was up until 1930, and then down again. There's no trend, *absolutely no trend.*

Another way of looking at what is going on is the tide gauge. Tide gauging is very complicated, because it gives different answers for wherever you are in the world. But we have to rely on geology when we interpret it. So, for example, those people in the IPCC [Intergovernmental Panel on Climate Change] choose Hong Kong, which has six tide gauges, and they choose the record of one, which gives 2.3 mm per year rise of sea level. Every geologist knows that that is a subsiding area. It's the compaction of sediment; it is the only record which you *shouldn't* use. And if that figure is correct, then Holland would not be subsiding, it would be uplifting. And that is just ridiculous. Not even ignorance could be responsible for a thing like that. So tide gauges, you have to treat very, very carefully.

Now, back to satellite altimetry, which shows the water, not just the coasts, but in the whole of the ocean. And you measure it by satellite. From 1992 to 2002, [the graph of the sea level] was a straight line, variability along a straight line, but absolutely no trend whatsoever. We could see those spikes: a very rapid rise, but then in half a year, they fall back again. But absolutely no trend, and to have a sea-level rise, you need a trend.

Then, in 2003, the same data set, which in their [IPCC's] publications, in their Web site, was a straight line—suddenly it changed, and showed a very strong line of uplift, 2.3 mm per year, the same as from the tide gauge. And that didn't look so nice. It looked as though they had recorded something; but they *hadn't* recorded anything. It was the original one which they had suddenly twisted up, because they entered a "correction factor," which they took from the tide gauge. So it was not a measured thing, but a figure introduced from outside. I accused them of this at the Academy of Sciences in Moscow—I said you have introduced factors from outside; it's not a measurement. It looks like it is measured from the satellite, but you don't say what really happened. And they answered, that we had to do it, because otherwise we would not have gotten any trend!

That is terrible! As a matter of fact, it is a falsification of the data set. Why? Because they know the answer. And there you come to the point: They "know" the answer; the rest of us, we are *searching* for the answer. Because we are field geologists; they are computer scientists. So all this talk that sea level is rising, this stems from the computer modeling, not from observations. The observations don't find it!

I have been the expert reviewer for the IPCC, both in 2000 and last year [2006]. The first time I read it, I was exceptionally surprised. First of all, it had 22 authors, but none of them—*none*—were sea-level specialists. They were given this mission because they promised to answer the right thing. Again, it was a computer issue. This is the typical thing: The meteorological community works with computers, simple computers. Geologists don't do that! We go out in the field and observe, and then we can try to make a model with computerization; but it's not the first thing.

So there we are. Then we went to the Maldives. I traced a drop in sea level in the 1970s, and the fishermen told me, "Yes, you are correct, because we remember"—things in their sailing routes have changed, things in their harbor have changed. I worked in the lagoon, I drilled in the sea, I drilled in lakes, I looked at the shore morphology—so many different environments. Always the same thing: In about 1970, the sea fell about 20 cm, for reasons involving probably evaporation or something. Not a change in volume or something like that—it was a rapid thing. The new level, which has been stable, has not changed in the last 35 years. You can trace it so very, very carefully. No rise at all is the answer there.

Another famous place is the Tuvalu Islands, which are supposed to soon disappear because they've put out too much carbon dioxide. There we have a tide gauge record, a variograph record, from 1978, so it's 30 years. And again, if you look there, *absolutely no trend*, no rise.

So, from where do they get this rise in the Tuvalu Islands?

Then we know that there was a Japanese pineapple industry which subtracted too much fresh water from the inland, and those islands have very little fresh water available from precipitation, rain. So, if you take out too much, you destroy the water magazine, and you bring sea water into the magazine, which is not nice. So they took out too much fresh water and in came salt water. And of course the local people were upset. But then it was much easier to say, "No, no! It's the global sea level rising! It has nothing to do with our subtraction of fresh water." So there you have it. This is a local industry which doesn't pay.

You have Vanuatu, and also in the Pacific, north of New Zealand and Fiji—there is the island Tegua. They said they had to evacuate it, because the sea level was rising. But again, you look at the tide-gauge record: There is absolutely no signal that the sea level is rising. If anything, you could say that maybe the tide is lowering a little bit, but absolutely no rising.

And again, where do they get it from? They get it from their inspiration, their hopes, their computer models, but not from observation. Which is terrible.

We have Venice. Venice is well known, because that area is techtonically, because of the delta, slowly subsiding. The rate

The Rate of Sea Level Rise Is Unlikely to Increase

Sea level (SL) rise is one of the most feared impacts of any future global warming, but public discussion of the problem is beset by poor data and extremely misleading analysis.

Eminent practitioners in the field have termed current estimates of SL rise a "puzzle," an "enigma," and even "fiction."

S. Fred Singer,
"Nature, Not Human Activity, Rules the Climate,"
The Heartland Institute, March 3, 2008. www.heartland.org.

has been constant over time. A rising sea level would immediately accelerate the flooding. And it would be so simple to record it. And if you look at that 300-year record: In the 20th Century it was going up and down, around the subsidence rate. In 1970, you should have an acceleration, but instead, the rise almost finished. So it was the opposite.

If you go around the globe, you find no rise anywhere. But they need the rise, because if there is no rise, there is no death threat. They say there is nothing good to come from a sea-level rise, only problems, coastal problems. If you have a temperature rise, if it's a problem in one area, it's beneficial in another area. But sea level is the real "bad guy," and therefore they have talked very much about it. But the real thing is, that it doesn't exist in observational data, only in computer modeling. . . .

How does the IPCC get these small island nations so worked up about worrying that they're going to be flooded tomorrow?

Because they get support, they get money, so their idea is to attract money from the industrial countries. And they believe that if the story is not sustained, they will lose it. So, they *love* this story. But the local people in the Maldives—it would be terrible to raise children—why should they go to school, if in 50 years everything will be gone? The only thing you should do, is learn how to swim.

To take your example of Tuvalu, it seems to be more of a case of how the water management is going on, rather than the sea level rising.

Yes, and it's much better to blame something else. Then they can wash their hands and say, "It's not our fault. It's the U.S., they're putting out too much carbon dioxide."

Which is laughable, this idea that CO_2 is driving global warming.

Precisely, that's another thing.

And like this *State of Fear*, by [author] Michael Crichton, when he talks about ice. Where is ice melting? Some Alpine glaciers are melting, others are advancing. Antarctic ice is certainly *not* melting; all the Antarctic records show *expansion* of ice. Greenland is the dark horse here for sure; the Arctic may be melting, but it doesn't matter, because they're already floating, and it has no effect. A glacier like Kilimanjaro, which is important, on the Equator, is *only* melting because of deforestation. At the foot of the Kilimanjaro, there was a rain forest; from the rain forest came moisture, from that came snow, and snow became ice. Now, they have cut down the rain forest, and instead of moisture, there comes heat; heat melts the ice, and there's no more snow to generate the ice. So it's a simple thing, but has nothing to do with temperature. It's the misbehavior of the people around the mountain. So again, it's like Tuvalu: We should say this deforestation, that's the thing. But instead they say, "No, no, it's the global warming!"

Here, over the last few days, there was a grouping that sent out a power-point presentation on melting glaciers, and how this is going to raise sea level and create all kinds of problems.

The only place that has that potential is Greenland, and Greenland east is not melting; Greenland west, the Disco Bay is melting, but it has been melting for 200 years, at least, and the rate of melting *decreased* in the last 50–100 years. So, that's another falsification.

But more important, in 5,000 years, the whole of the Northern Hemisphere experienced warming, the Holocene Warm Optimum, and it was 2.5 degrees warmer than today. And still, no problem with Antarctica, or with Greenland; still, no higher sea level.

These scare stories are being used for political purposes.

Yes. Again, this is for me, the line of demarcation between the meteorological community and us: They work with computers; we geologists work with observations, and the observations do not fit with these scenarios. So what should you change? We cannot change observations, so we have to change the scenarios!

Instead of doing this, they give an endless amount of money to the side which agrees with the IPCC. The European Community, which has gone far in this thing: If you want a grant for a research project in climatology, it is written into the document that there *must* be a focus on global warming. All the rest of us, we can never get a coin there, because we are not fulfilling the basic obligations. That is really bad, because then you start asking for the answer you want to get. That's what dictatorships did, autocracies. They demanded that scientists produce what they wanted.

Increasingly science is going in this direction, including in the nuclear industry—it's like playing computer games. It's like the design of the Audi, which was done by computer, but not tested in reality, and it flipped over. They didn't care about physical principles.

You frighten a lot of scientists. If they say that climate is not changing, they lose their research grants. And some people cannot afford that; they become silent, or a few of us speak up, because we think that it's for the honesty of science, that we have to do it.

In one of your papers, you mentioned how the expansion of sea level changed the earth's rotation into different modes—that was quite an eye-opener.

Yes, but it is exceptionally hard to get these papers published also. The publishers compare it to IPCC's modeling, and say, "Oh, this isn't the IPCC." Well, luckily it's not! But you cannot say that.

What were you telling me the other day, about 22 authors being from Austria?

Three of them were from Austria, where there is not even a coast! The others were not specialists. So that's why, when I became president of the INQUA Commission on Sea-Level Change and Coastal Evolution, we made a research project, and we had this up for discussion at five international meetings. And all the true sea level specialists agreed on this figure, that in 100 years, we might have a rise of 10 cm, with an uncertainty of plus or minus 10 cm—that's not very much. And in recent years, I even improved it, by considering also that we're going into a cold phase in 40 years. That gives 5 cm rise, plus or minus a few centimeters. That's our best estimate. But that's very, very different from the IPCC statement.

Ours is just a continuation of the pattern of sea level going back in time. Then you have absolutely maximum figures, like when we had all the ice in the vanishing ice caps that happened to be too far south in latitude after the Ice Age. You couldn't have more melting than after the Ice Age. You reach up to 10 mm per year—that was the *super*-maximum: 1 meter in 100 years. Hudson Bay, in a very short period, melted away: it came up to 12 mm per year. But these are so exceptionally large, that we cannot be anywhere *near* it; but still people have been saying, 1 meter, 3 meters. It's not feasible! These are figures which are so large, that only when the ice caps were vanishing, did we have those types of rates. They are absolutely extreme. This frame is set by the maximum-maximum rate, and we have to be far, far lower. We are basing ourselves on the observations—in the past, in the present, and then predicting it into the future, with the best of the "feet on the ground" data that we can get, not from the computer.

Isn't some of what people are talking about just shoreline erosion, as opposed to sea-level rise?

Yes, and I have very nice pictures of it. If you have a coast, with some stability of the sea level, the waves make a kind of equilibrium profile—what they are transporting into the sea and what they are transporting onshore. If the sea rises a little, yes, it attacks, but the attack is not so vigorous. On the other hand, if the sea goes down, it is eating away at the old equilibrium level. There is a much larger redistribution of sand.

We had an island, where there was heavy erosion, everything was falling into the sea, trees and so on. But if you looked at what happened: The sand which disappeared there, if the sea level had gone up, that sand would have been placed higher, on top of the previous land. But it is being placed below the previous beach. We can see the previous beach, and it is 20–30 cm above the current beach. So this is erosion because the sea level *fell*, not because the sea level *rose*. And it is more common that erosion is caused by falling sea level, than by rising sea level.

| "This makes agriculture the leading source of impairment in the Nation's rivers and lakes, and a major source of impairment in estuaries."

Agriculture Threatens Water Quality

Marc Ribaudo and Robert Johansson

In the following viewpoint, Marc Ribaudo and Robert Johansson maintain that agricultural operations are one of the biggest threats to water quality in the United States. Ribaudo and Johansson say that livestock and crop farms cause several forms of water pollution. Lakes, rivers, and underground aquifers that are located near farms are contaminated with sediment, nitrogen from fertilizers, phosphorus and bacteria from animal manure, and other agricultural pollutants that seriously degrade water quality. The authors assert that controlling agricultural water pollution is a difficult and significant challenge for states and the federal government. Ribaudo and Johansson are scientists at the U.S. Department of Agriculture's Economic Research Service.

Marc Ribaudo and Robert Johansson, *Agricultural Resources and Environmental Indicators*, 2006 Edition. Washington, DC: Economic Research Service, United States Department of Agriculture, 2006. www.ers.usda.gov.

As you read, consider the following questions:

1. According to Ribaudo and Johansson, the significance of water pollutants commonly produced by agriculture is suggested by information from whom and in accordance with what statute?

2. According to Ribaudo and Johansson, the major concern for surface water quality is eutrophication, which can result in what?

3. What do Ribaudo and Johansson say is the primary reason that controlling agricultural pollution is such a challenge?

The production practices and inputs used by agriculture can result in a number of pollutants entering water resources, including *sediment, nutrients, pathogens, pesticides, and salts.* Farmers, when making production decisions, often do not consider offsite impacts associated with runoff or leaching. Documenting the links between agriculture and water quality can help policy makers provide appropriate incentives to farmers for controlling pollution that originates on farms.

Studies Show Agriculture Is Major Source of Water Pollution

Agriculture is widely believed to have significant impacts on water quality. While no comprehensive national study of agriculture and water quality has been conducted, the magnitude of the impacts can be inferred from several water quality assessments. A general assessment of water quality is provided by EPA's [U.S. Environmental Protection Agency's] 2000 Water Quality Inventory. Based on State assessments of 19 percent of river and stream miles, 43 percent of lake acres, and 36 percent of estuarine square miles, EPA concluded that agriculture is the leading source of pollution in 48 percent of river miles,

41 percent of lake acres (excluding the Great Lakes), and 18 percent of estuarine waters found to be water-quality impaired, in that they do not support designated uses. This makes agriculture the leading source of impairment in the Nation's rivers and lakes, and a major source of impairment in estuaries. Agriculture's contribution has remained relatively unchanged over the past decade.

The significance of water pollutants commonly produced by agriculture is suggested by information on impaired waters provided by States, tribes, and territories to EPA in accordance with Section 303(d) of the Clean Water Act. These are waters that do not meet water quality standards, and cannot meet those standards through point-source controls alone. The most recent information (2005) indicates that 25,823 bodies of water (stream reaches or lakes) are impaired nationwide. Pathogens, sediment, and nutrients are among the top sources of impairment, and agriculture is a major source of these pollutants in many areas.

A U.S. Geological Survey (USGS) study of agricultural land in watersheds [an extent of land where water drains downhill into a body of water, also called a drainage basin] with poor water quality estimated that 71 percent of U.S. cropland (nearly 300 million acres) is located in watersheds where the concentration of at least one of four common surface-water contaminants (nitrate, phosphorus, fecal coliform bacteria, and suspended sediment) exceeded generally accepted instream criteria for supporting water-based recreation activities. Another USGS study found that structural changes in animal agriculture between 1982 and 1997 put upward pressure on stream concentrations of fecal coliform bacteria in many areas of the Great Plains, Ozarks, and Carolinas.

Sediment from Soil Erosion

Sediment is the largest contaminant of surface water by weight and volume and is identified by States as the second leading pollution problem in rivers and streams and the third leading problem in lakes. Sediment in surface water is largely a result of soil erosion, which is influenced by soil properties and the production practices farmers choose. Sediment buildup reduces the useful life of reservoirs. Sediment can clog roadside ditches and irrigation canals, block navigation channels, and increase dredging costs. By raising streambeds and burying streamside wetlands, sediment increases the probability and severity of floods. Suspended sediment can increase the cost of water treatment for municipal and industrial water uses. Sediment can also destroy or degrade aquatic wildlife habitat, reducing diversity and damaging commercial and recreational fisheries.

Regions with the greatest potential to discharge sediment from cropland to surface waters include parts of the Heartland, Mississippi Portal, and Prairie Gateway.

Nitrogen and Phosphorus from Fertilizers and Manure

Nitrogen and *phosphorus* are important crop nutrients, and farmers apply large amounts to cropland each year. They can enter water resources through runoff and leaching. The major concern for surface-water quality is the promotion of algae growth (known as eutrophication), which can result in decreased oxygen levels, fish kills, clogged pipelines, and reduced recreational opportunities. USGS has found that high concentrations of nitrogen in agricultural streams are correlated with nitrogen inputs from fertilizers and manure used on crops and from livestock waste. Nine percent of domestic wells sampled by USGS's National Water-Quality Assessment Program (NAWQA) during 1993–2000 had nitrate concentrations exceeding EPA's drinking water standard (maximum contaminant level or MCL) of 10 milligrams per liter, and agriculture was identified as the major source. EPA reported in its Water Quality Inventory that nutrient pollution is the leading cause of water quality impairment in lakes and a major cause of oxygen depletion in estuaries.

Watersheds with a high potential to deliver nitrogen to surface water are primarily in the Heartland and Southern Seaboard regions. Watersheds with a high potential to discharge nitrogen to ground water are primarily in the Southern Seaboard, Fruitful Rim, Heartland, and Prairie Gateway regions. Watersheds with a high potential to discharge phosphorus to surface water are located primarily in the Heartland, Southern Seaboard, and Northern Crescent regions.

Eutrophication and hypoxia (low oxygen levels) in the northern Gulf of Mexico have been linked to nitrogen loadings from the Mississippi River. Agricultural sources (fertilizer, soil inorganic nitrogen, and manure) are estimated to contribute about 65 percent of the nitrogen loads entering the Gulf from the Mississippi Basin. As much as 15 percent of the nitrogen fertilizer applied to cropland in the Mississippi River Basin makes its way to the Gulf of Mexico.

The Gulf of Mexico is not the only coastal area affected by nutrients. Recent research by the National Oceanographic and Atmospheric Administration has found that 44 estuaries (40 percent of major U.S. estuaries) exhibit highly eutrophic conditions, caused primarily by nitrogen enrichment. These conditions occur in estuaries along all coasts, but are most prevalent in estuaries along the Gulf of Mexico and Mid-Atlantic coasts. Watersheds with a high potential to discharge nitrogen from agriculture to estuaries are located primarily in the Heartland, Mississippi Portal, and Southern Seaboard regions.

Pesticides Applied on Farmland

Farmers apply a wide variety of *pesticides* to control insects (insecticides), weeds (herbicides), fungus (fungicides), and other problems. Well over 500 million pounds (active ingredient) of pesticides have been applied annually on farmland since the 1980s, and certain chemicals can travel far from where they are applied. Pesticide residues reaching surface-water systems may harm freshwater and marine organisms, damaging recreational and commercial fisheries. Pesticides in drinking water supplies may also pose risks to human health. At least one of seven prevalent herbicides was found in 37 percent of the groundwater sites examined by USGS as part of the National Water-Quality Assessment Program, but all at low concentrations.

Watersheds with a high propensity to discharge pesticides to surface water are located primarily in the Heartland and Mississippi Portal regions. Watersheds with a high propensity to discharge pesticides to ground water are primarily in the Heartland, Prairie Gateway, and Southern Seaboard regions.

Salts from Irrigation Water

Some irrigation water applied to cropland may run off the field into ditches and to receiving waters. These irrigation return flows often carry *dissolved salts* as well as nutrients and pesticides into surface or ground water. Increased salinity levels in irrigation water can reduce crop yields or damage soils such that some crops can no longer be grown. Increased concentrations of naturally occurring toxic minerals—such as selenium, molybdenum, and boron—can harm aquatic wildlife and impair water-based recreation. Increased levels of dissolved solids in public drinking water supplies can increase water treatment costs, force the development of alternative water supplies, and reduce the lifespans of water-using household appliances.

Dissolved salts and other minerals are a significant cause of pollution in the Prairie Gateway and arid portions of the Fruitful Rim and Basin and Range. Selenium is of particular concern because of its adverse biological effects. Selenium in irrigation return flows was identified as the cause of mortality, congenital deformities, and reproductive failures in aquatic birds in Kesterson Reservoir in western San Joaquin Valley,

Factory Farms Threaten Public Health

On most factory farms, animals are crowded into relatively small areas; their manure and urine are funneled into massive waste lagoons. These cesspools often break, leak or overflow, sending dangerous microbes, nitrate pollution and drug-resistant bacteria into water supplies. Factory-farm lagoons also emit toxic gases such as ammonia, hydrogen sulfide and methane. What's more, the farms often spray the manure onto land, ostensibly as fertilizer—these "sprayfields" bring still more of these harmful substances into our air and water.

Natural Resources Defense Council,
"Pollution from Giant Livestock Farms Threatens Public Health,"
July 15, 2005. www.nrdc.org.

California. A Department of Interior study of the Western United States found that 4,100 square miles of land irrigated for agriculture is susceptible to selenium contamination, along with adjacent land that may receive return flows. Affected areas are primarily in California, western Kansas, eastern Colorado, and western South Dakota.

Pathogens from Livestock Waste

The possibility of *pathogens* contaminating water supplies and recreation waters is a continuing concern. Bacteria are the largest source of impairment in rivers and streams, according to EPA's water quality inventory. Potential sources include inadequately treated human waste, wildlife, and animal feeding operations. Diseases from micro-organisms in livestock waste can be contracted through direct contact with contaminated water, consumption of contaminated drinking water, or consumption of contaminated shellfish. Bacterial, rickettsial, viral, fungal, and parasitic diseases are potentially transmissible from livestock to humans. Fortunately, proper animal management practices and water treatment minimize this risk. However, protozoan parasites, especially *Cryptosporidium* and *Giardia*, are important sources of waterborne disease outbreaks. *Cryptosporidium* and *Giardia* may cause gastrointestinal illness, and *Cryptosporidium* may lead to death in persons with compromised immune systems. These parasites have been commonly found in beef herds and *Cryptosporidium* is widespread on dairy operations.

Government Control of Agricultural Water Pollution, a Challenge

While agriculture's impacts on water resources are widespread and considered to be significant, the control of agricultural pollution is a challenge. The primary reason for this is that pollution from agriculture is generally "nonpoint" in nature. Nonpoint-source pollution has four characteristics that have an important bearing on the design of policies for reducing it.

- Nonpoint emissions are generated diffusely over a broad land area. These emissions leave from fields in so many places that it is generally not cost effective to accurately monitor emissions using current technology.

- Nonpoint emissions (and their transport to water or other resources) are subject to significant natural variability due to weather-related events and other environmental characteristics.

- Nonpoint emissions and the associated water quality impacts depend on many site-specific characteristics, such as soil type, topography, proximity to the water resource, climate, etc.

- Nonpoint pollution problems are often characterized by a very large number of nonpoint polluters.

The difficulties in measurement, variability of discharges, and the site-specific nature make regulations used for point sources (factories and sewage treatment plants) largely inappropriate for nonpoint sources. As a consequence, water quality laws such as the Clean Water Act generally do not regulate agricultural pollution, but, instead, pass most of the responsibility on to the States. This has resulted in quite varied responses, reflecting the States' particular resource concerns and organizational capacity. Thirty-three States have laws with provisions that regulate agriculture under certain conditions, such as when voluntary approaches fail to achieve water quality goals. States commonly use technology standards that require farmers to implement conservation plans that contain recommended management practices, such as conservation tillage, nutrient management, pesticide management, and irrigation water management. These plans can be required statewide, or in areas particularly vulnerable to agricultural pollution.

By contrast, the Federal Government relies primarily on voluntary approaches, such as education and financial assistance (policy instruments), to encourage farmers to protect water quality. Major USDA [United States Department of Agriculture] programs such as the Environmental Quality Incentive Program and Conservation Security Program are important sources of information and assistance for farmers concerned with water quality.

| "Farm and ranch lands provide food and cover for wildlife, help control flooding, protect wetlands and watersheds, and maintain air quality."

Agriculture Can Benefit the Environment and Water Quality

American Farmland Trust

In the following viewpoint, American Farmland Trust (AFT) asserts that U.S. agriculture provides many benefits, including helping to improve water quality. According to AFT, U.S. agriculture is at risk. Each year, fewer farms exist than the year before, primarily as a result of increasing urban development. AFT says that agriculture provides many benefits to America and that these benefits are lost when agricultural land is developed. According to AFT, one of the benefits of well-managed agricultural land is the protection of watersheds. AFT believes that development causes many more detrimental impacts on water quality than agriculture does. American Farmland Trust is a nonprofit organization formed in 1980 by farmers and conservationists to protect America's agricultural resources.

American Farmland Trust, "Fact Sheet: Why Save Farmland?" Washington, DC: American Farmland Trust—Farmland Information Center, 2003. Reproduced by permission. www.farmland.org.

As you read, consider the following questions:

1. According to the USDA's [United States Department of Agriculture'] National Resources Inventory, how many acres of rural land were converted to developed land between 1992 and 1997?

2. According to AFT, development increases pollutants that lead to groundwater contamination. What are some of these increased pollutants?

3. According to AFT, "managed" open spaces of farmland and ranch land provide opportunities for what kind of activities?

Fertile soils take thousands of years to develop. Creating them takes a combination of climate, geology, biology and good luck. So far, no one has found a way to manufacture them. Thus, productive agricultural land is a finite and irreplaceable natural resource.

America's agricultural land provides the nation—and world—with an unparalleled abundance of food and fiber products. The dominant role of U.S. agriculture in the global economy has been likened to OPEC's [Organization of the Petroleum Exporting Countries] in the field of energy. The food and farming system is important to the balance of trade and the employment of nearly 23 million people. Across the country, farmland supports the economic base of many rural and suburban communities.

Agricultural land also supplies products with little market value, but enormous cultural and ecological importance. Some are more immediate, such as social heritage, scenic views, open space and community character. Long-range environmental benefits include wildlife habitat, clean air and water, flood control, groundwater recharge and carbon sequestration.

Yet despite its importance to individual communities, the nation and the world, American farmland is at risk. It is imperiled by poorly planned development, especially in urban-influenced areas, and by the complex forces driving conversion. USDA's [United States Department of Agriculture's] Economic Research Service (ERS) developed "urban influence" codes to classify each of the nation's 3,141 counties and county equivalents into groups that describe the degree of urban influence. AFT [American Farmland Trust] found that in 1997, farms in the 1,210 most urban-influenced counties produced 63 percent of dairy products and 86 percent of fruits and vegetables.

According to USDA's National Resources Inventory (NRI), from 1992 to 1997 more than 11 million acres of rural land were converted to developed use—and more than half of that conversion was agricultural land. In that period, an average of more than 1 million agricultural acres were developed each year. And the rate is increasing—up 51 percent from the rate reported in the previous decade.

Agricultural land is desirable for building because it tends to be flat, well drained and generally is more affordable to developers than to farmers and ranchers. Far more farmland is being converted than is necessary to provide housing for a growing population. Over the past 20 years, the acreage per person for new housing almost doubled. Most of this land is outside of existing urban areas. Since 1994, lots of 10 to 22 acres accounted for 55 percent of the growth in housing area. The NRI shows that the best agricultural soils are being developed fastest.

The U.S. food and farming system contributes nearly $1 trillion to the national economy—or more than 13 percent of the gross domestic product—and employs 17 percent of the labor force. With a rapidly increasing world population and expanding global markets, saving American farmland is a prudent investment in world food supply and economic opportunity.

Asian and Latin American countries are the most significant consumers of U.S. agricultural exports. Latin America, including Mexico, purchases an average of about $10.6 billion of U.S. agricultural exports each year. Asian countries purchase an average of $23.6 billion/year, with Japan alone accounting for about $10 billion/year. Even as worldwide demand for a more diverse diet increases, many countries are paving their arable land to support rapidly expanding economies. Important customers today, they are expected to purchase more agricultural products in the future.

While domestic food shortages are unlikely in the short term, the U.S. Census predicts the population will grow by 42 percent in the next 50 years. Many developing nations already are concerned about food security. Of the 78 million people currently added to the world each year, 95 percent live in less developed regions. The productivity and diversity of American agriculture can ensure food supplies and continuing preeminence in world markets. But this depends upon an investment strategy that preserves valuable assets, including agricultural land, to supply rapidly changing global demand.

Saving farmland is an investment in community infrastructure and economic development. It supports local government budgets and the ability to create wealth locally. In addition, distinctive agricultural landscapes are often magnets for tourism.

People vacation in the state of Vermont or Steamboat Springs, Colo., because they enjoy the scenery created by rural meadows and grazing livestock. In Lancaster, Pa., agriculture is still the leading industry, but with the Amish and Mennonites working in the fields, tourism is not far behind. Napa Valley, Calif., is another place known as a destination for "agro tourism." Tourists have become such a large part of most Napa Valley wineries that many vintners have hired hospitality staff. Both the valley and the wines have gained name recognition, and the economy is thriving.

Agriculture contributes to local economies directly through sales, job creation, support services and businesses, and also by supplying lucrative secondary markets such as food processing. Planning for agriculture and protecting farmland provide flexibility for growth and development, offering a hedge against fragmented suburban development while supporting a diversified economic base.

Development imposes direct costs to communities, as well as indirect costs associated with the loss of rural lands and open space. Privately owned and managed agricultural land generates more in local tax revenues than it costs in services. Carefully examining local budgets in Cost of Community Services (COCS) studies shows that nationwide farm, forest and open lands more than pay for the municipal services they require, while taxes on residential uses consistently fail to cover costs. Related studies measuring the effect of all types of development on municipal tax bills find that tax bills generally go up as communities become more developed. Even those communities with the most taxable commercial and industrial properties have higher-than-average taxes.

Local governments are discovering that they cannot afford to pay the price of unplanned development. Converting productive agricultural land to developed uses creates negative economic and environmental impacts. For example, from the mid-1980s to the mid-1990s, the population of Atlanta, Ga., grew at about the same rate as that of Portland, Ore. Due to its strong growth management law, Portland increased in size by only 2 percent while Atlanta doubled in size. To accommodate its sprawling growth, Atlanta raised property taxes 22 percent while Portland lowered property taxes by 29 percent. Vehicle miles traveled (and related impacts) increased 17 percent in Atlanta but only 2 percent in Portland.

Well-managed agricultural land supplies important non-market goods and services. Farm and ranch lands provide food and cover for wildlife, help control flooding, protect wetlands and watersheds, and maintain air quality. They can absorb and filter wastewater and provide groundwater recharge. New energy crops even have the potential to replace fossil fuels.

The federal government owns 402 million acres of forests, parks and wildlife refuges that provide substantial habitat for wildlife. Most of this land is located in 11 western states. States, municipalities and other non-federal units of government also own land. Yet public agencies alone cannot sustain wildlife populations. Well-managed, privately owned agricultural land is a critical resource for wildlife habitat.

With nearly 1 billion acres of land in farms, agriculture is America's dominant land use. So it is not surprising that farming has a significant ecological impact. Ever since the publication of Rachel Carson's *Silent Spring*, environmentalists have called attention to the negative impacts of industrial agricultural practices. However, converting farmland to development has detrimental long-term impacts on environmental quality.

Water pollution from urban development is well documented. Development increases pollution of rivers and streams, as well as the risk of flooding. Paved roads and roofs collect and pass storm water directly into drains instead of filtering it naturally through the soil. Septic systems for low-density subdivisions can add untreated wastes to surface water and groundwater—potentially yielding higher nutrient loads than livestock operations. Development often produces more sediment and heavy metal contamination than farming does and increases pollutants—such as road salt, oil leaks from automobiles and runoff from lawn chemicals—that lead to groundwater contamination. It also decreases recharge of aquifers, lowers drinking-water quality and reduces biodiversity in streams.

Urban development is a significant cause of wetland loss. Between 1992 and 1997, NRI showed that development was responsible for 49 percent of the total loss. Increased use of automobiles leads to traffic congestion and air pollution. Development fragments and often destroys wildlife habitat, and fragmentation is considered a principal threat to biodiversity.

Keeping land available for agriculture while improving farm management practices offers the greatest potential to produce or regain environmental and social benefits while minimizing negative impacts. From wetland management to on-farm composting for municipalities, farmers are finding ways to improve environmental quality.

To many people, the most compelling reasons for saving farmland are local and personal, and much of the political support for farmland protection is driven by grassroots community efforts. Sometimes the most important qualities are the hardest to quantify—such as local heritage and sense of place. Farm and ranch land maintain scenic, cultural and historic landscapes. Their managed open spaces provide beautiful views and opportunities for hunting and fishing, horseback riding, skiing, dirt-biking and other recreational activities. Farms and ranches create identifiable and unique community character and add to the quality of life. Perhaps it is for these reasons that the contingent valuation studies typically find that people are willing to pay to protect agricultural land from development.

Finally, farming is an integral part of our heritage and our identity as a people. American democracy is rooted in an agricultural past and founded on the principle that all people can own property and earn a living from the land. The ongoing relationship with the agricultural landscape connects Americans to history and to the natural world. Our land is our legacy, both as we look back to the past and as we consider what we have of value to pass on to future generations.

Public awareness of the multiple benefits of working lands has led to greater community appreciation of the importance of keeping land open for fiscal, economic and environmental reasons. As a result, people increasingly are challenging the perspective that new development is necessarily the most desirable use of agricultural land—especially in rural communities and communities undergoing transition from rural to suburban.

| "The breadth, depth and frequency of these invasions are facilitating what some scientists call 'invasional meltdown.'"

Invasive Species Are a Major Threat to the Great Lakes

Andy Buchsbaum

In the following viewpoint, Andy Buchsbaum asserts that the Great Lakes, which form the largest surface freshwater system on Earth, are in peril and invasive species are their biggest threat. According to Buchsbaum, invasive species, toxic pollution, shoreline development, and nutrient loading (discharges of phosphorus and nitrogen into the Lakes) are stressing the Lakes so much that the natural "immune system" or buffering capacity of the Lakes is drastically disabled. Buchsbaum believes that invasive species such as zebra and quagga mussels, sea lamprey, and viral hemorrhagic septicemia are the biggest sources of stress to the Great Lakes. These invasive species are linked with a massive decline in the Lakes' population of Diporeia *and other tiny creatures that make up the foundation of the food web. If something isn't done to stop new invaders from entering the Lakes, Buchs-*

Andy Buchsbaum, "Testimony Before the House Committee on Transportation and Infrastructure's Subcommittee on Water Resources and the Environment, Hearing on the Impact of Invasive Species," March 7, 2008. www.healthylakes.org. Reproduced by permission of the author.

baum says the Lakes may suffer irreparable damage. Buchsbaum is the director of the National Wildlife Federation's Great Lakes Office. His viewpoint is an excerpt of his testimony to a U.S. congressional committee, in which he asks for the federal government's help in protecting the Great Lakes from invasive species.

As you read, consider the following questions:

1. According to Buchsbaum, why was the report titled *Prescription for the Great Lakes Ecosystem Protection and Restoration* a surprise to the public?

2. According to Buchsbaum, since 1950, how often does one new invasive species enter the Great Lakes?

3. According to Buchsbaum, 99 percent of the foundation of the Great Lakes food web is composed of what four tiny species?

4. According to Buchsbaum, which invasive species that hasn't yet arrived in the Great Lakes could potentially be the worst one yet?

Despite their vast size, the Great Lakes are fragile and need our nation's help. In recent years, the Great Lakes have been increasingly plagued by beach closings due to untreated sewage; invasions by harmful exotic species (on average, one new invasive species enters the Great Lakes every seven months); contamination of sport and commercial fisheries; and loss of habitat for wildlife. Each of these and other problems have been viewed as a separate challenge to be researched and addressed independently; few have tried to assess the condition of the Great Lakes as an ecosystem and design solutions on that basis.

A Crisis of Historic Proportions

In December 2005, over sixty of the leading scientists in the Great Lakes region issued an alarming report. In a paper titled

Prescription for Great Lakes Ecosystem Protection and Restoration, the scientists concluded that the Great Lakes are experiencing a historic crisis. Deterioration of large sections of their ecosystem is accelerating dramatically, and if not addressed now, the damage is likely to be irreversible. In their own words:

> "There is widespread agreement that the Great Lakes presently are exhibiting symptoms of extreme stress from a combination of sources that include toxic contaminants, invasive species, nutrient loading, shoreline and upland land use changes, and hydrologic modifications. . . . In large areas of the lakes, historical sources of stress have combined with new ones to reach a *tipping point,* the point at which ecosystem-level changes occur rapidly and unexpectedly, confounding the traditional relationships between sources of stress and the expected ecosystem response. *There is compelling evidence that in many parts of the Great Lakes we are beyond this tipping point. Certain areas of the Great Lakes are increasingly experiencing ecosystem breakdown,* where intensifying levels of stress from a combination of sources have overwhelmed the natural processes that normally stabilize and buffer the system from permanent change."

Over 200 scientists from around the country, including from California, Hawaii and Tennessee, have endorsed the report.

The scientists' report was a surprise to the public because to many, the Great Lakes and their tributaries seem to be improving. Due to fundamental policy shifts like the Clean Water Act, massive government investment in better sewers and responsible private initiatives, rivers no longer catch fire, Lake Erie has come back from the dead, the water often looks clearer and many pollutant indicators have improved. But such observations only scratch the surface and the scientists looked much deeper to find an ecosystem in crisis. They have documented:

- The destruction of the foundation of the Great Lakes food web in many of the Great Lakes. Populations of the basic food group for most fish, freshwater shrimp called *Diporeia*, have declined from over 10,000 per square meter of lake bottom to virtually zero over vast stretches of Lake Michigan and the other Great Lakes. The scientists cannot be sure, but they believe the decline is linked to the infestation of the Great Lakes by an invasive species, the zebra mussel, which colonizes the lakebeds in thick mats of shells that extend for acres and leaves the surrounding lakebeds barren of life. The National Wildlife Federation produced a report describing the devastating impact that invasive species have had on the Great Lakes in a report titled *Ecosystem Shock*.

- Lake Erie's so-called "dead zone," an area deprived of oxygen, has reappeared in central Lake Erie. Accompanying this anoxic zone is the return elsewhere in the lake of blue-green (toxic) algae blooms and episodic die-offs of fish and fish-eating birds from avian botulism. Scientists are seeing similar eutrophication problems in Lake Huron's Saginaw Bay and Lake Michigan's Green Bay.

- Many fish populations are showing signs of stress and decline in the Great Lakes. Scientists have found widespread decline in growth, condition and numbers of yellow perch, lake whitefish and other valuable fish species in Lake Michigan and portions of Lake Huron.

The scientists concluded that these and other large-scale ecosystem changes result from the loss of the Great Lakes' capacity to buffer themselves against sources of stress—essentially, damage to the Great Lakes immune system. Much of the buffering capacity for the Great Lakes comes from healthy near-shore communities and tributaries. As these areas are damaged by pollution, hydrologic modifications, invasive spe-

One Way Invasive Species Get into the Great Lakes

With growing international trade, there are increases in the amount and frequency of ballast water transfers [water that is from another port or location and taken on-board a ship in order to add weight and stability], and associated organisms, between distant ports.

Ballast water discharges from vessels on international and domestic voyages can contribute to the spread of invasive species in the U.S.

U.S. Environmental Protection Agency,
"Fact Sheet: Ballast Water and Aquatic Invasive Species,"
October 2005. www.epa.gov.

cies and shoreline development, they lose their capacity to buffer the Great Lakes. Without that buffering capacity, each new stress—whether it is an invasive species or additional pollution—can set off a cascade of damage to the ecosystem that occurs rapidly and unexpectedly. In the scientists' words:

"In the Great Lakes, nonlinear changes are no longer a future threat—these types of changes are taking place now. While in some areas some indicators of ecosystem health have continued to improve over the past decade, other large areas of the lakes are undergoing rapid changes where combinations of effects of old and new stresses are interacting synergistically to trigger *a chain reaction process of ecosystem degradation. The rapidness of this chain-reaction process, seen over the past five to fifteen years and involving sudden and unpredicted changes, is unique in Great Lakes recorded history.*"

Invasive Species Are Biggest Threat

Although it is hard to determine which problem is the largest cause of the ecosystem breakdowns now plaguing the Great Lakes, many scientists believe that it is invasive species. It is easy to see why:

- Scientists have found 183 aquatic invasive species in the Great Lakes thus far, making it one of the most invaded ecosystems in the world. They include:

- Eel-like sea lamprey that attack lake trout and suck the blood out of them;

- Zebra and quagga mussels that form thick mats of shells over vast stretches of the lake floors and beaches and disrupt the food chain;

- A fish-killing virus called viral hemorrhagic septicemia that has spread to Lakes Ontario, Erie and Huron and caused multiple fish kills; and

- Most recently, bug-eyed shrimp that feed on tiny zooplankton and phytoplankton that directly or indirectly sustain the Great Lakes native fish species was found in Lake Michigan.

- Since 1950, on average one new invasive species has entered the Great Lakes every seven months. Under such an onslaught it is impossible to conceive of how the Great Lakes ecosystem could possibly reach any sort of equilibrium, how aquatic life could recover or how scientists and managers could make decisions to help restore the lakes' buffering capacity.

- Invasive species are affecting every level of the Great Lakes ecosystem: the lake bottoms, the water column, the surface, the shorelines, the near shore and the open water, the zooplankton, the forage fish and the fish at the top of the food web (like trout and walleye).

- The breadth, depth and frequency of these invasions are facilitating what some scientists call "invasional meltdown." Some invaders alter their new environment in ways that make it easier for subsequent invaders to thrive, making it even more difficult for native species to survive.

- The aquatic invaders are only one part of the invasives problem. Terrestrial invaders also are having devastating impacts on the Great Lakes ecosystem, making restoration more difficult and raising the costs. All along the coastlines and tributaries, the wetlands so important for the Great Lakes immune system are being taken over by phragmites and purple loosestrife. Lake Ontario is losing its native wetlands, which are based on sedge grasses. As we propose to spend billions of dollars on restoring coastal wetlands, we need to protect the wetlands we have from these terrestrial invaders.

Damage to the Food Web

Virtually every ecosystem breakdown in the Great Lakes identified by the scientists—the Lake Erie anoxic zone, the declines and stresses in fish populations, and widespread food web disruption—are caused in large part by invasive species. The massive damage to the Great Lakes food web over the past 15 years is perhaps the most illustrative example of why invasive species are so devastating. Fully 99 percent of the foundation of the food web—the food available to fish in the sediments of the Great Lakes—is made up of four species: tiny shrimp-like creatures called *Diporeia*; fingernail clams; certain worms, and opossum shrimp. Of these, *Diporeia*, the tiny shrimp, dominate making up 80 percent of the available food.

Since about 1990, however, the *Diporeia* and fingernail clam populations have crashed over vast stretches of Lake Michigan, Lake Huron and other lakes. . . . Dr. Tom Nalepa of NOAA's [National Atmospheric and Oceanic Administration's] Great Lakes Environmental Research Laboratory, based on his research of the past two decades, . . . show a 94 percent decline in *Diporeia* organisms in Lake Michigan over 10 years and a 57 percent decline of those organisms in Lake Huron in only 3 years. *Diporeia* populations have gone from 10,000 organisms per square meter to virtually zero in many areas. Scientists have also seen a parallel crash in the populations of fingernail clams, and are now concerned about the viability of the other major food source, the opossum shrimp.

Scientists believe that the cause of this collapse is zebra mussels. Zebra mussels colonize the lakebeds in thick mats of shells that extend for acres and leave the surrounding lakebeds barren of life. They are not completely sure, though, and are still searching for the mechanism that causes the disappearance of the *Diporeia*.

Ironically, zebra mussel populations are now declining in the Great Lakes. The invasive quagga mussel is crowding them out. The quagga mussel threatens to further depress the *Diporeia* populations in the Great Lakes, and even worse, decimate the remaining food sources in the lake sediments— particularly the opossum shrimp. . . .

The damage to these foundation species is sending waves throughout the Great Lakes food web. We are seeing impacts on native perch, walleye and trout. Combined with the other invasive species that have invaded our region, the Great Lakes ecosystem is experiencing breakdown. As invasive species like zebra and quagga mussels overwhelm the Great Lakes, large stretches of the lakes that used to be teeming with life are now barren.

These rapid and dramatic changes to the Great Lakes food web are unprecedented in the recorded history of the lakes.

And unless we take action now, the attacks on the lakes will only worsen. The damage to the food web done by zebra mussels, quagga mussels and other aquatic invaders will be very difficult to repair.

Unless we stop new invaders from entering the Great Lakes, however, restoring them will be impossible. The Great Lakes cannot even begin to recover when every seven months another invasive species enters the lakes and begins to wreak its own particular kind of havoc on the ecosystem. Scientists say they are falling farther and farther behind in even understanding the lakes because the system changes so dramatically due to these fresh invasions.

Monster Fish May Be on the Way and Threaten More Damage

Potentially the worst aquatic invaders to the Great Lakes thankfully have not yet arrived. They are Asian and silver carp, large fish with voracious appetites that are only 50 miles from Lake Michigan. These fish can grow as large as 100 pounds and six feet in length and eat everything in their path. They were intentionally introduced to clean out catfish farms on the Mississippi, but escaped and migrated up the Mississippi River to the Chicago Sanitary and Ship Canal. In some areas of the Mississippi River, Asian carp have multiplied so rapidly that in less than a decade they make up 90 percent or more of the fish life. Scientists at the Illinois Department of Natural Resources have shown that native fish are suffering. The average weight of a 25-inch buffalo fish, a native and popular fish with locals in the Illinois River, has dropped from over 12 pounds to less than 9 pounds over five years.

The only thing standing between these monster fish and Lake Michigan is a temporary underwater electric barrier installed by the U.S. Army Corps of Engineers [in 2002]. Unfortunately, a permanent barrier has design problems and cannot be brought on-line without further investment and time, and the temporary barrier is not failsafe. Until the permanent barriers are operational and effective, the Great Lakes are at extreme risk. As a U.S. Fish and Wildlife officer explained to a newspaper, "If the Asian carp get into Lake Michigan, they will turn the Great Lakes into giant carp ponds."

▌ *"Most invasions do no harm."*

Not All Invasive Species Are Bad

Alan Burdick

In the following viewpoint, Alan Burdick asserts that invasive species are generally harmless. Burdick traces the idea that invasive species are harmful to English ecologist Charles Elton, who postulated that invasive species were like a disease infecting ecosystems. Burdick says that no evidence of this exists. He contends that ecosystems can generally accommodate and make room for invasive species. According to Burdick, invasive species don't cause ecosystems to collapse, shrink, or disappear. Burdick writes for numerous publications including The New York Times Magazine *and* Natural History. *He is the author of the book* Out of Eden: An Odyssey of Ecological Invasion.

As you read, consider the following questions:

1. According to Burdick, we are on the verge of a new era, in which the greatest threat to biological diversity is nature itself. What does one scientist call this new era?

2. What is the name of the 1958 book by Charles Elton that represented the first scientific study of invasions, according to Burdick?

3. Did zoologists Heather Hager and Karen McCoy find much evidence to suggest that invasions of purple loose-strife have any serious ecological consequences?

I have seen the future, and it lives in Miami.

The suburbs of Miami, to be exact: in the ever-expanding netherworld between the potted plants and subtropical night-life of South Beach to the east and the tropical plants and deep-rooted, wildlife of Everglades National Park to the west.

The future lives in Homestead. So does Todd Hardwick, owner and primary employee of Pesky Critters Nuisance Wild-life Control. Noisome possums and trash-can raccoons are his standard fare, and the money is in alligators, which crawl out of the swamps and into backyards, the two environments be-ing ever more synonymous. But the real fun, and Hardwick's specialty, is catching exotic species. Miami is the through point of the nation's imported animal and plant trade, and virtually everyone in South Florida, including Hardwick, has a neighbor with a backyard menagerie of lucrative critters on hold for resale. With so many unofficial zoos so close together and so little expertise at maintaining them, animals are con-stantly escaping into the streets and flower beds, and when someone spots, say, a pesky cougar on the lawn, Hardwick gets the call.

A Melting Pot of Species

Hardwick has caught mountain lions, ostriches, rheas, emus, macaque monkeys—even, once, a bison on the freeway. Mostly the animals are lone escapees, but a number of species—especially reptiles—have gone loose often enough that they've formed free-roaming populations that reproduce amid the imported mango groves and ornamental hedgerows. The naturalized aliens include Cuban tree frogs, various South American anoles, and South Asian pythons and boa constrictors. Hardwick's business card shows a photograph of an Indonesian python he once extracted from a burrow beneath someone's home; it was 22 feet long.

In short, if all the biogeographic barriers in the world were suddenly eliminated—all the impassable gulfs, oceans, and mountain ranges that have historically kept the planet's local native species from moving around and mixing together—the jumbled result would look something like Homestead. Minus the lions and pythons, it's the sort of neighborhood into which we're all slowly moving—or is slowly moving into ours. Colonies of stinging South American fire ants have settled in Texas, the zebra mussel, a pistachio-size mollusk from Europe, carpets the bottom of the Great Lakes. Feral pigs, native to Eurasia and North Africa, now root in the lawns of San Jose, California. Giant Asian carp, introduced in the 1970s to control aquatic weeds, leap unsolicited into fishing boats along the Mississippi River. Escaped pets, sport fish and garden plants run amok, insects that come hidden in the foliage of imported plants, pests that are introduced to control other pests—the invaders are legion, from anywhere, going everywhere.

Nature appears to be entering a new era—the Homogecene, one scientist calls it—wherein the greatest threat to biological diversity is no longer just bulldozers or pesticides but, in a sense, nature itself. The renowned Harvard biologist Edward O. Wilson has claimed that the introduction of alien species is second only to habitat destruction as the leading cause of extinctions worldwide. A recent NASA [National Aeronautics and Space Administration] report, heralding a novel effort to monitor the progress of alien species via satellite, placed the economic cost of alien species between $100 billion and $200 billion. "Nonindigenous invasive species may pose the single most formidable threat of natural disaster of the 21st century," the report's authors warn. "The threat of invasive species is perhaps our most urgent economic and conservation challenge." Purple loosestrife, that showy Eurasian flower you may have seen advancing along roadsides? Its floral path leads straight to hell.

Or not. Like the outwardly pastoral streets of Homestead, nothing is quite what meets the eye when it comes to alien species. For the past 50 years ecologists have devoted close study to movements of exotic species, in an effort to better understand why they go where they do and the impact they have when they arrive. The results of this unintended natural experiment turn out to be surprising, even to scientists. Nature, it seems, is far more resilient and is run by ecological rules that are far less orderly than expected. Alien species do pose a threat. But their real crime isn't against nature; it's against us and our self-serving ideas of what nature is supposed to be.

Invasive Species, Like a Disease?

The scientific study of invasions dates to 1958, with the publication of *The Ecology of Invasions by Animals and Plants* by the English ecologist Charles Elton. "We must make no mistake," he wrote. "We are seeing one of the great historical convulsions in the world's fauna and flora." Elton and his followers sought to discern underlying patterns of invasion, to forge theories about the hidden structures of ecosystems, and so explain the apparent patterns of invasions. Are some organisms better invaders than others? Why do American gray squirrels seem to be everywhere? Why do certain environments, notably islands like Hawaii, seem especially vulnerable to invasion? Every invasion was a potential case study in why ecosystems do—and don't—remain intact.

As Elton saw it, an ecosystem is analogous to a human community, with a limited number of job openings, or niches.

"When an ecologist says, 'There goes a badger,'" Elton wrote, "he should include in his thoughts some definite idea of the animal's place in the community to which it belongs, just as if he had said, 'There goes the vicar.'" The secret ingredient determining the composition of any given ecosystem—who's in, who's out—is competition. Every species, native or alien, must vie for limited niche space, like a game of musical chairs or like mailmen battling over access to a handful of mail slots.

For Elton and many subsequent ecologists, this explained why places like Hawaii were unusually vulnerable to the incursion of alien species. Small ecosystems are simpler—with fewer species, and thus more available niches—and so are more open to new species. Also, the native residents of these small ecosystems—surrounded by fewer species than their counterparts in large continental ecosystems—are evolutionarily less fit to compete against invaders. "The balance of relatively simple communities of plants and animals is more easily upset than that of richer ones," he wrote, "and more vulnerable to invasions." For confirmation, look no further than the average vacant lot or agricultural plot: low in diversity and highly invaded.

Elton was among, the first natural scientists to articulate a link between biological diversity—the number and variety of native species in an ecosystem—and ecological health. Greater diversity conveys a degree of "biotic resistance," he argued, which helps preserve the integrity of an ecosystem over time. A natural, undisturbed ecosystem could be thought of as an immunologic system; invasion, its disease. A recent issue of *National Geographic* described ecological invasion as a "green cancer."

The disease metaphor is compelling. There's just one problem: Fifty years of research by invasion biologists around the world has failed to confirm it.

Invasives Really Aren't Better Competitors

When an alien species enters a new ecosystem, it can alter the environment in a number of ways: by eating native species (in its 50 years on Guam, the Australian brown tree snake has eliminated 9 of 13 native bird species); by spreading disease among them (introduced birds in Hawaii thrive in part because they are far less susceptible to the avian malaria parasite, also an introduced species, than native birds are); or by altering the environment in such a way that favors themselves (like melaleuca, an Australian tree that is spreading through the Everglades in part by changing the frequency and intensity of fires).

What invading species mostly don't do, it turns out, is outcompete native species. Take the case of the American gray squirrel, which was introduced in England in 1876. Dubbed "tree rat" by its detractors, the invader has made a pest of itself in its new land, where it is in the habit of eating flower bulbs and birds' eggs and stripping the bark from young birch trees. In addition, the spread of the gray squirrel has coincided with declining numbers of the Eurasian red squirrel, a native beloved by Brits despite the fact that it is only slightly less destructive than the gray squirrel.

Over the years, the gray squirrel has become an almost iconic example of an invading species outcompeting a native one. But even with fewer than 30,000 red squirrels remaining in England today, there is little hard proof that competition explains the gray squirrel's success or the red squirrel's decline. Scientists have found that the gray is more efficient at foraging in the woods and in backyards. On the other hand, even before the gray's arrival, red squirrel populations in Britain had a periodic tendency to die out. (They were reintroduced to Scotland and Ireland several times during the 19th century.) In addition, it is now known that two-thirds of gray squirrels are silent carriers of a viral skin disease fatal to red squirrels. Domination comes easier to those who can spread a pox. But is that competition?

By and large, superior competitive ability isn't what enables alien species to invade. Likewise, small ecosystems can't be said to be competitively weaker than big ones. Small ecosystems are more vulnerable to extinctions; their member species are fewer in number and have limited refuge, and so are at statistically greater risk of being eliminated by a single event, whether a hurricane or the introduction of a predatory snake. But biological diversity per se—the number of species in an ecosystem—provides no shield against invasions. In a 1999 issue of the journal *Biological Invasions*, Daniel Simberloff, a prominent ecologist at the Institute for Biological Invasions at the University of Tennessee at Knoxville, writes simply, "It seems clear to me that there is no prima facie [literally 'on its first appearance'] case for the biotic resistance paradigm."

There's Generally Extra Room at the Inn

Indeed, one of the big surprises to invasion biologists is the large number of alien species that any given ecosystem can harbor. South Florida, perhaps the most conspicuously invaded region on the U.S. mainland, is home to at least 300 introduced plant species—about 18 percent of the plant total. In San Francisco Bay, marine ecologists Jim Carlton of the Maritime Studies Program of Williams College and Mystic Seaport and Andrew Cohen of the San Francisco Estuary Institute have discovered more than 250 nonindigenous species. In the classic view of ecosystems, outlined by Elton and later Robert MacArthur and E.O. Wilson in their theory of island biogeography, ecosystems run on a knife's edge: They are tightly structured, without much room for new competitors.

"What invasions have shown is that there are plenty of unused resources," says Ted Grosholz, a marine biologist at the University of California at Davis who for years has monitored the incursion of the European green crab into the bay. "Ecosystems can absorb a lot of new species. I mean, holy cow, look at San Francisco Bay! Who would have thought an ecosystem had that much unused niche space?"

Invasions unfold invisibly. The average person will take alarm at a lion in the street—a large novelty and a personal hazard—but pay less heed to the progress of Asian crabgrass and Cuban tree frogs in the backyard ("Honey, is that a toad?"). Most alien species blend seamlessly into the ecosystems they enter. Like wallflowers, they slip in quietly, hang around the margins, and keep to themselves.

Which isn't to say that a wallflower will necessarily remain a wallflower. The Brazilian pepper tree, introduced into South Florida a century ago, began to spread widely only in the 1950s; it now fills significant portions of the Everglades, in part by exuding a poisonous sap and clearing space for itself. And once an alien species becomes widespread, it is extremely difficult to eliminate.

Most Invasions Are Harmless

Still, most invasions do no harm. Even prevalent ones can have surprisingly little impact on their new environments. A review of the history of purple loosestrife by zoologists Heather Hager and Karen McCoy, formerly at the University of Guelph in Ontario, concluded that despite belief to the contrary, there is little or no evidence to suggest that the incursion of the plant has serious ecological consequences. "The direct scientific rationale used to advocate purple loosestrife control does not exist," they write, adding that "aesthetic reasons remain the justification for its control."

Marine environments turn out to be particularly absorbent to—and forgiving of—alien species. Although exotic crabs, sea worms, sponges, clams, and diseases have been introduced around the world for hundreds of years on or in ships (and by many other means), marine biologists have documented not a single example of an invading marine species driving a native marine species extinct, whether by predation, competition, or disease.

"The key question is, what is the impact?" says Grosholz. "What effect does it have? Does it matter? Extinction may not be the only issue. That's the main difference between marine and terrestrial ecosystems. With the Australian brown tree snake in Guam you can point to species and say, 'Look, those things are gone.' With marine species it's not so easy. You can get qualitative shifts in communities if a species falls below a certain population threshold. I'm more concerned about those kinds of changes."

Invasion is not a zero-sum game, with invaders replacing natives at a one-to-one (or a one-to-two, or more) ratio. Rather, and with critical exceptions, it is a sum-sum game, in which ecosystems can accept more and more species. Indeed, in both marine and terrestrial ecosystems, the big surprise is that the incursion of alien species can actually increase, rather than decrease, biodiversity at a local level. This makes sense: If you add many new species and subtract no or only a few native ones, the overall species count goes up.

To put it differently, invasions don't cause ecosystems to collapse. That's what Florida illustrates so vividly. If anything, there's more nature running around there than ever before. In small ecosystems like the Everglades or the Hawaiian Islands, where native species are already imperiled by disappearing habitat, invading species may be the final straw. Invasions may radically alter the components of an ecosystem, perhaps to a point at which the ecosystem becomes less valuable, engaging, or useful to humans. But unlike, say, the clear-cutting of a forest or the poisoning of a lake, invasions don't make ecosystems shrink or disappear.

Periodical Bibliography

Farmers Guardian   "Farmers and Experts Unite to Face Pollution Challenge," March 6, 2009.

David Festa   "Bringing Oceans to a Boil," *USA Today*, September 2008.

Rick Jervis, William M. Welch, and Richard Wolf   "Worth the Risk? Debate on Offshore Drilling Heats Up," *USA Today*, July 14, 2008.

Jessica A. Knoblauch   "Troubled Waters: 'Ocean Deserts' Are Expanding, Disrupting Habitats and Suffocating Marine Life," *Our Planet*, October 27, 2008.

Richard H. Moore, Jason Shaw Parker, and Mark Weaver   "Agricultural Sustainability, Water Pollution, and Governmental Regulations: Lessons from the Sugar Creek Farmers in Ohio," *Culture & Agriculture*, 2008.

New Scientist   "Early Warning of Disastrous Climate Change Could Come from Underwater Gliders Patrolling the Oceans," November 29, 2008.

Jeff Poor   "Nightly News Jumps Onboard Mercury-in-Fish Alarmism," *Business & Media Institute*, December 31, 2008. www.businessandmedia.org.

Laura Sayre   "The Hidden Link Between Factory Farms and Human Illness," *Mother Earth News*, February–March 2009.

Tatyana Sinitsyna   "Lake Baikal Faces Multiple Threats," *Moscow News*, April 3, 2009.

J.T. Trevors and M.H. Saier   "Where Is the Global Environmental Bailout?" *Water, Air & Soil Pollution*, 2009.

Kevin E. Trenberth   "Warmer Oceans, Stronger Hurricanes," *Scientific American*, 2007.

U.S. News & World Report   "How Global Warming Threatens Millions in Bangladesh," March 26, 2009.

Is There a Water Crisis?

Chapter Preface

An iconic picture of the developing world is that of a young woman carrying a large container on her head. Years ago the container was made of clay or stone. In the twenty-first century it is more than likely made of plastic. What's inside the container, however, hasn't changed for hundreds of years—it's water. Most people in developed regions of the world—Europe, North America, East Asia—take water for granted. They use it for drinking, bathing, sanitation, watering the garden, and even recreation. Swimming pools are a common site in suburban American neighborhoods. In developing regions of the world, however, water cannot be taken for granted. A staggering number of people worldwide do not have access to clean water for drinking or water for sanitation.

About 16 percent of people worldwide lack access to safe drinking water, causing hardship, disease, and poverty and exacerbating gender inequalities. According to the United Nations in 2006, 1.1 billion people lacked access to an "improved source of water." This means they obtained water for drinking, cooking, and other uses directly from a river or pond, an unprotected well or spring, or from water vendors, whom typically sell unsafe water at exorbitant prices.

Unimproved drinking water, like water from a river or pond, has a high probability of being contaminated with pathogenic bacteria and viruses. Because of a lack of sanitation facilities, human excrement, loaded with pathogenic microorganisms, contaminates the same rivers and ponds people use for drinking. Drinking water contamination also occurs because of a lack of water for proper hygiene, such as simple hand washing.

Easily preventable, infectious waterborne diseases such as cholera, typhoid, guinea worm disease, and diarrhea are responsible for 80 percent of illnesses and deaths in the developing world, many of them children. Cholera—a dreaded disease of centuries past—is now extremely rare in the United States and other developed countries. However, cholera epidemics are common in sub-Saharan Africa. According to Eric Mintz, leader of the U.S. Centers for Disease Control (CDC) diarrheal diseases epidemiology team, and Richard Guerrant, director of Global Health at the University of Virginia School of Medicine, "Inexcusably, the completely preventable ancient scourge of cholera rages among poverty-stricken and displaced people today, with as many as one in five persons with severe illness dying for lack of safe drinking water and sanitation and a simple therapy consisting of salt, sugar, and water." In 2007, guinea worm disease sickened thousands of people in Ghana and Sudan. Guinea worm disease is an extremely painful waterborne infection characterized by thread-like worms slowly emerging from the human body through blisters. Children are most susceptible to diarrheal infections—millions of children in developing countries die every year from diarrhea. According to Rochelle Rainey, from the U.S. Agency for International Development (USAID), "International attention can be lacking for the thousands of children who die every day from diarrhea, even though solutions are available to greatly reduce this tragedy." Rainey also says that children who survive an episode of diarrhea face problems later in life. She says, "Diarrhea and poor nutrition have lifelong effects for children, leading directly to decreased physical and cognitive development." According to experts like Mintz and Rainey, most waterborne diseases in the developing world could easily be prevented by merely adding a couple of drops of bleach to a family's water supply.

Women and children are often the hardest hit by not having access to water. Women are primarily responsible for obtaining water for a family's needs. Women in Africa and other developing countries typically walk a half-mile or more to obtain water for their family—often traveling through unsafe areas making them vulnerable to attacks from animals and men. They typically carry five gallons of water on their head— about forty-two pounds—and make the half mile trip six or seven times a day. The time women spend looking for water cuts into the time they have to care for their children, prepare food, and participate in other activities. According to Joke Muylwijk, executive director of the Gender Water Alliance, "There are some women who spend their whole lives looking for water."

Women often rely on their daughters to help look for water and thus perpetuate their unequal status in the next generation. According to the United Nations and UNICEF (United Nations Children's Fund) one in five girls of primary-school age are not in school, compared to one in six boys. In addition to their responsibilities of looking for water, menstruating girls also stay away from schools because the schools typically do not have toilets or latrines.

Lack of sanitation is as equally devastating as the lack of clean, drinking water for people in the developing world. According to a 2008 report by the World Health Organization and UNICEF, 30 percent of the world's population lacks access to a sanitation facility that ensures hygienic separation of human excreta from human contact. This includes 18 percent of people worldwide who practice open defecation. Forty-eight percent or those in Southern Asia and 28 percent of those in sub-Saharan Africa have nowhere to relieve themselves, except out in the open. Where open defecation is the rule, menstruating women and girls often wait until dusk or night to relieve themselves. Just as when they travel to find water, this makes them vulnerable to attacks by animals and men.

The lack of access to safe drinking water and sanitation is a serious problem in the developing world. Some people are worried because they think the world itself is running out of access to clean fresh drinking water. If this occurred it would clearly exacerbate the situation in the developing world. There are other people, however, who believe that fresh water is abundant on Earth, but must be managed more efficiently. Still other people believe that there are ways to increase the world's supply of safe drinking water, such as desalinating the oceans. The authors in the following chapter provide various opinions on the state of the world's water and whether or not there is a water crisis.

> *"The confident blue lines in a million atlases simply do not tell the truth about rivers sucked dry, for the most part, to irrigate food crops."*

Water Scarcity Is Creating a Global Food Crisis

Fred Pearce

In the following viewpoint, Fred Pearce contends that water scarcity is creating a global food crisis. Pearce says that inefficient agricultural activities are literally sucking the earth's rivers and underground aquifers dry. According to Pearce, nations with relatively abundant sources of water used to be able to feed the drier, more arid regions of the world. This is no longer the case, however, due to droughts in major food exporting countries and population growth in China and other places. Pearce doesn't believe that the earth contains enough water to feed the burgeoning human population. He believes water scarcity will cause a global food crisis. Pearce is an author and journalist in the United Kingdom.

As you read, consider the following questions:

1. According to Pearce, what are the two underlying causes of the current crisis over world food prices?

2. According to Pearce, in the last fifteen years, how many pumps have Indians purchased to tap underground water supplies?

3. Which country is the largest net supplier of virtual water, according to a UNESCO [United Nations Educational, Scientific, and Cultural Organization] report? Which one is the largest gross supplier of virtual water?

After decades in the doldrums, food prices have been soaring this year [2008], causing more misery for the world's poor than any credit crunch. The geopolitical shockwaves have spread round the world, with food riots in Haiti, strikes over rice shortages in Bangladesh, tortilla wars in Mexico, and protests over bread prices in Egypt.

The immediate cause is declining grain stocks, which have encouraged speculators, hoarders, and panic-buyers. But what are the underlying trends that have sown the seeds for this perfect food storm?

Biofuels are part of it, clearly. A quarter of U.S. corn is now converted to ethanol, powering vehicles rather than filling stomachs or fattening livestock. And the rising oil prices that encouraged the biofuels boom are also raising food prices by making fertilizer, pesticides, and transport more expensive.

But there is something else going on that has hardly been mentioned, and that some believe is the great slow-burning, and hopelessly underreported, resource crisis of the 21st century: water.

Climate change, overconsumption and the alarmingly inefficient use of this most basic raw material are all to blame. I wrote a book three years ago titled *When The Rivers Run Dry*. It probed why the Yellow River in China, the Rio Grande and

Colorado in the United States, the Nile in Egypt, the Indus in Pakistan, the Amu Darya in Central Asia, and many others are all running on empty. The confident blue lines in a million atlases simply do not tell the truth about rivers sucked dry, for the most part, to irrigate food crops.

We are using these rivers to death. And we are also pumping out underground water reserves almost everywhere in the world. With two-thirds of the water abstracted from nature going to irrigate crops—a figure that rises above 90 percent in many arid countries—water shortages equal food shortages.

Consider the two underlying causes of the current crisis over world food prices: falling supplies from some of the major agricultural regions that supply world markets, and rising demand in booming economies like China and India.

Why falling supplies? Farm yields per hectare have been stagnating in many countries for a while now. The green revolution that caused yields to soar 20 years ago may be faltering. But the immediate trigger, according to most analysts, has been droughts, particularly in Australia, one of the word's largest grain exporters, but also in some other major suppliers, like Ukraine. Australia's wheat exports were 60 percent down last year; its rice exports were 90 percent down.

Why rising demand? China has received most of the blame here—its growing wealth is certainly raising demand, especially as richer citizens eat more meat. But China traditionally has always fed itself—what's different now is that the world's most populous country is no longer able to produce all its own food.

A few years ago, the American agronomist and environmentalist Lester Brown wrote a book called *Who Will Feed China?: Wake Up Call for a Small Planet*. It predicted just this. China can no longer feed itself largely because demand is rising sharply at a time when every last drop of water in the north of the country, its major breadbasket, is already taken.

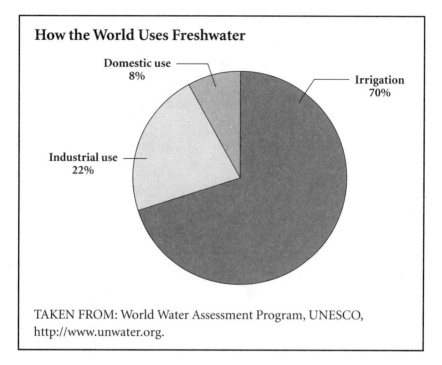

How the World Uses Freshwater

Domestic use
8%

Irrigation
70%

Industrial use
22%

TAKEN FROM: World Water Assessment Program, UNESCO,
http://www.unwater.org.

The Yellow River, which drains most of the region, now rarely reaches the sea, except for the short monsoon season.

Some press reports have recently suggested that China is being sucked dry to provide water for the [2008] Beijing Olympics.

Would that it were so simple. The Olympics will require only trivial amounts of water. China's water shortages are deep-seated, escalating, and tied to agriculture. Even hugely expensive plans to bring water from the wetter south to the arid north will only provide marginal relief.

The same is true of India, the world's second most populous country. Forty years ago, India was a basket case. Millions died in famines. The green revolution then turned India into a food exporter. Its neighbor Bangladesh came to rely on India for rice. But Indian food production has stagnated recently, even as demand from richer residents has soared. And the main reason is water.

With river water fully used, Indian farmers have been trying to increase supplies by tapping underground reserves. In
the last 15 years, they have bought a staggering 20 million
Yamaha pumps to suck water from beneath their fields. Tush-
aar Shah, director of the International Water Management
Institute's groundwater research station in Gujarat, estimates
those farmers are pumping annually to the surface 100 cubic
kilometers more water than the monsoon rains replace. Water
tables are plunging, and in many places water supplies are giving out.

"We are living hand-to-mouth," says D.P. Singh, president
of the All India Grain Exporters Association, who blames water shortages for faltering grain production. Last year India
began to import rice, notably from Australia. This year, it
stopped supplying its densely populated neighbor Bangladesh,
triggering a crisis there too.

More and more countries are up against the limits of food
production because they are up against the limits of water
supply. Most of the Middle East reached this point years ago.
In Egypt, where bread riots occurred this spring, the Nile
River no longer reaches the sea because all of its water is
taken for irrigation.

A map of world food trade increasingly looks like a map
of the water haves and have-nots, because in recent years the
global food trade has become almost a proxy trade in water—or rather, the water needed to grow food. "Virtual water,"
some economists call it. The trade has kept the hungry in dry
lands fed. But now that system is breaking down, because
there are too many buyers and not enough sellers.

According to estimates by UNESCO's [United Nations
Educational, Scientific, and Cultural Organization'] hydrology
institute, the world's largest net supplier of virtual water until
recently was Australia. It exported a staggering 70 cubic kilometers of water a year in the form of crops, mainly food.

With the Murray-Darling Basin, Australia's main farming zone, virtually dry for the past two years, that figure has been cut in half.

The largest gross exporter of virtual water is the United States, but its exports have also slumped as corn is diverted to domestic biofuels, and because of continuing drought in the American West.

The current water shortages should not mark an absolute limit to food production around the world. But it should do three things. It should encourage a rethinking of biofuels, which are themselves major water guzzlers. It should prompt an expanding trade in food exported from countries that remain in water surplus, such as Brazil. And it should trigger much greater efforts everywhere to use water more efficiently.

On a trip to Australia in the midst of the 2006 drought, I was staggered to see that farmers even in the most arid areas still irrigate their fields mostly by flooding them. Until the water runs out, that is. Few have adopted much more efficient drip irrigation systems, where water is delivered down pipes and discharged close to roots. And, while many farmers are expert at collecting any rain that falls on their land, they sometimes allow half of that water to evaporate from the surfaces of their farm reservoirs.

For too long, we have seen water as a cheap and unlimited resource. Those days are coming to an end—not just in dry places, but everywhere. For if the current world food crisis shows anything, it is that in an era of global trade in "virtual water," local water shortages can reverberate throughout the world—creating higher food prices and food shortages everywhere.

> *"My own research suggests that the situation may not be as dire as many are suggesting."*

Water Scarcity Is Exaggerated

Jonathan Chenoweth

In the following viewpoint, Jonathan Chenoweth asserts that there is enough water on the earth for all nations to enjoy a high quality of life. He sees reports of water scarcity as being a bit exaggerated and off the mark. According to Chenoweth, global food trading has meant that countries with scant water resources can avoid agriculture—and most importantly avoid agriculture's vast water consumption—by importing food from water rich areas. This so-called virtual water trading means that water from dry areas can be used for drinking water and other needs rather than agriculture. Chenoweth believes that virtual water allows countries to get by with minimal amounts of water if it is properly managed. There is enough water to go around, says Chenoweth. Chenoweth is a scientist at the Centre for Environmental Strategy at the University of Surrey in the United Kingdom.

As you read, consider the following questions:

1. According to Chenoweth, the definitions of water scarcity used by the United Nations and others were proposed in 1986 by whom?

2. According to the UN Food and Agriculture Organization (FAO), what percentage of the 43,750 cubic kilometers of fresh water returned each year to the earth's rivers, lakes, and aquifers is currently extracted?

3. How many liters of fresh water (per person per day) does Chenoweth conclude is the bare minimum that will allow a country to prosper?

Today's focus on the credit crisis and rising prices for food and oil has temporarily put another global scarcity in the shade: water. The UN [United Nations] predicts that by 2025, two-thirds of us will experience water shortages, with severe lack of water blighting the lives and livelihoods of 1.8 billion. According to the UN World Water Assessment Programme, by 2050, 7 billion people in 60 countries may have to cope with water scarcity. At this year's [2008] World Economic Forum, UN secretary-general Ban Ki-moon recommended that water scarcity should be at the top of the international agenda. "As the global economy grows, so will its thirst," he said, warning of a future marred by conflicts over water.

Rethinking What Water Scarcity Means

There is no doubt that we need to rethink how we use water, especially with the human population growing rapidly, and global warming likely to produce unpredictable patterns of rainfall and drought. Nevertheless, my own research suggests that the situation may not be as dire as many are suggesting. Nations can thrive on surprisingly meagre quantities of fresh water—provided they adopt water-efficient technologies and encourage economic activity that doesn't guzzle water. I be-

lieve the looming water crisis is primarily a problem of distribution and management rather than supply. And we can solve
it with existing technologies, increased investment and political will.

The definitions of water scarcity most widely accepted and
used today by the UN and others were proposed in 1986 by
Malin Falkenmark, then at the Swedish Natural Sciences Research Council. She defined a country as "water-stressed"
when it cannot extract more than 4654 litres of water per person per day (equivalent to 1700 cubic metres per person per
year) from its rivers and aquifers. One with less than 2738 litres available per person Falkenmark classified as "water-
scarce". Anything below 1369 litres constitutes "absolute water
scarcity", and threatens economic development as well as human health and well-being.

Most of the Middle East is already classified as being water-
scarce according to these definitions, but perhaps more surprisingly so are Malta and Singapore, while Denmark, Poland
and the Czech Republic are classed as water-stressed. In total,
approximately 290 million people live in countries that are
classed as water-scarce, and another 440 million live in countries that are water-stressed. However, I believe these bench-
marks need to be re-examined, and when that is done, a very
different picture emerges.

The main problem with Falkenmark's figures is that they
refer to the amount of water required for a country to be self-
sufficient in food production in a semi-arid region. Agriculture is among the most water-intensive human activities, particularly where crops need irrigation. According to the report
Water Footprints of Nations, published in 2004 by the
UNESCO-IHE Institute for Water Education, producing a ki-
logram of wheat takes more than 1300 litres of water, for example. For rice, the figure is almost 3000 litres.

However, such self-sufficiency is no longer essential because the global food supply is much more integrated than it

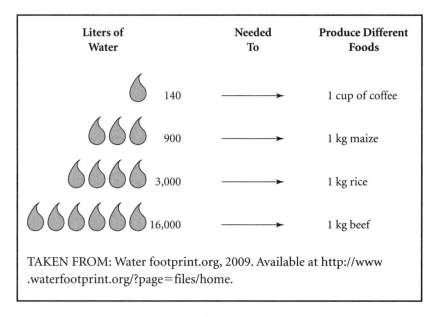

Liters of Water		Needed To	Produce Different Foods
140		$\longrightarrow$	1 cup of coffee
900		$\longrightarrow$	1 kg maize
3,000		$\longrightarrow$	1 kg rice
16,000		$\longrightarrow$	1 kg beef

TAKEN FROM: Water footprint.org, 2009. Available at http://www .waterfootprint.org/?page=files/home.

was even 20 years ago. Research by Tony Allan at King's College London, for example, reveals that countries across the Middle East have increasingly compensated for water scarcity by importing grains grown elsewhere. Allan coined the term "virtual water" to describe this trade, since the imports substitute for water that would otherwise be required locally to grow crops. Recent figures from the UN Food and Agriculture Organization (FAO) show the trend of rapidly increasing global trade of "virtual water". Between 1970 and 2001, food trade increased 60 percent in calorie terms.

Virtual Water: Breaking the Link Between Local Water Resources and Food

Some of the world's least developed countries now participate in the global food trade, breaking the link between local water resources and food security. Figures from the FAO show that in 2002, imports made up a fifth of the grain supply across sub-Saharan Africa, the region with the lowest average national incomes in the world, with food aid making up less than a fifth of the total food imports in least developed countries. Since the 1960s the world's least developed countries have changed from being net exporters to being significant net importers of agricultural commodities, and hence have become major importers of virtual water, even though most are not particularly short of water.

Of course, trade in virtual water does not reduce overall demand for water but rather shifts it from one place to another. However, with such a growing trade in virtual water, it no longer makes sense to use self-sufficiency in food production to define water scarcity. As with so many other commodities that are traded globally, self-sufficiency in food production is not a requirement for individual countries so long as water resources remain adequate at the global level, in the same way that so many countries are heavily dependent on the global oil trade, without which their economies would grind to a halt.

Globally, there is adequate fresh water available, and that looks set to continue in the long term. Figures from the FAO indicate that we currently extract less than 10 percent of the 43,750 cubic kilometres of fresh water returned each year to Earth's rivers, lakes and aquifers. The water is not distributed evenly, of course. Within a given country water consumption can vary from less than 1 percent of available resources to more than 100 percent, meaning that in some cases resources are being overexploited and degraded. Nevertheless, countries such as France, Germany, Italy and Spain have all shown that it is possible to extract 20 percent or more of renewable water resources a year while maintaining acceptable environmental quality. Globally we are still some way from hitting any real environmental ceiling on consumption, and the growing trade in virtual water means that scarcity in one region can be compensated for by increased production in places with more plentiful supplies.

I am also dubious that water scarcity, as defined by Falkenmark, determines a country's economic development. My own comparison of basic indicators of human, social and economic development with national water availability reveals no such relationship. Knowing the size of a country's fresh water resources does not allow you to predict how developed it is. In many desert states in the Middle East, for example, you will never lack safe drinking water, whereas in many water-rich countries in Africa you will.

How Much Water Does a Country Need?

So how much water does a country really need? The lowest estimate on the table is just 20 litres per person per day, put forward by Guy Howard at the UK Department for International Development and Jamie Bartram at the World Health Organization in Geneva. This figure, however considers only the water required for drinking, cooking and very basic hygiene. My own assessment, . . . considers domestic, agricultural and commercial water use, and aims to show how much fresh water a country needs to provide its people with a decent standard of living—and it puts a very different perspective on the global water crisis.

Any calculation of this kind is bound to involve value judgements, such as what level of development is adequate and what sort of development is acceptable. Although far from perfect as a measure of whether a country provides its people with a decent standard of living, the Human Development Index established by the UN Development Programme is arguably the best global indicator now available. It combines various measurements of health, education and wealth to provide a broad overview of development, ascribing countries such as Qatar, Mexico and Tonga a high level of development alongside countries more commonly considered developed.

With this as my starting point, I examined domestic water usage in countries with high levels of human development to get an idea of how little water people can get by on in their homes and still have a decent standard of living. FAO figures indicate that of highly developed countries, the Netherlands, the UK and Uruguay are the most water-efficient. People there use fewer than 100 litres a day, compared with more than 700 litres in New Zealand and Canada, which have the highest consumption among highly developed countries. . . .

Next, I considered non-domestic water usage. In countries with high human development, the amount used in the industrial and service sectors (excluding agriculture) ranges from just over 3 litres of water per person per day in Malta to more than 2800 litres in Canada and Bulgaria, according to the FAO. . . .

I also looked at water consumption within different economic sectors to find out how a country with limited water resources of its own might still maintain a healthy economy. While few countries publish such information it is available from the UK's National Statistics agency. This shows that the UK's service sector consumes just 30 litres per head of population per day—less than 4 percent of the country's total water usage—yet contributes nearly 80 percent of national wealth. Add in other water-efficient sectors such as construction and electrical equipment manufacturing, and you find that 90 percent of the UK's economic activity uses just 34 litres per person per day.

Nations Can Thrive with a Minimum of Water

Admittedly there are also water-hungry sectors such as chemicals manufacturing, textiles and paper, but a country with scarce water supplies could steer its economy away from these areas and rely on trade. The concept of virtual water increasingly encompasses these products as well as food. By importing virtual water, a nation could offer a high quality of life with as little as 135 litres of water per person per day—allowing 85 litres for household needs and assuming a well-maintained water supply system with distribution losses of around 10 percent.

If 135 litres is the bare minimum that will allow a country to prosper, where does that leave us? At present, only Kuwait and the United Arab Emirates fall short of this low-water mark in terms of their naturally available renewable water resources, but both make up their shortfall through desalination, and human development in both of these countries is already classed as high.

Even countries without oil wealth have shown that water scarcity need not impede development. For example, FAO figures show that Malta has just 346 litres of extractable water per person per day, while the Bahamas has just 183 litres of water per person per day. Both have already achieved high human development.

Plentiful water is clearly beneficial for national development, and it is imperative that total water resources remain sufficient for global food production. However, the fundamental problem many nations face is not water scarcity but distribution both within countries and between them.

Nevertheless, there are positive signs that we can overcome these problems. According to the WHO [World Health Organization] and UNICEF [United Nations Children's Fund], between 1990 and 2002 the percentage of the global population with access to safe drinking water rose from 77 to 83 percent. Meanwhile, the trade in virtual water continues to grow, shifting agricultural production from areas of water scarcity to those with relative plenty. Governments are also starting to rethink their water management policies—although admittedly these are still often fragmented and contradictory. What's more, with desalination now as cheap as 50 cents per 1000 litres, all but the world's least developed countries can afford to supplement their natural supplies of fresh water as long as they have a coastline. Millions are suffering because of a lack of water, but ensuring the supply of 135 litres per person per day is not beyond our reach.

> *"In a corner of the world already fraught with tense rivalries, control over the most basic human resource is almost certain to be a cause for violent conflict."*

Armed Conflicts Will Arise over Water Scarcity

Alex Stonehill

In the following viewpoint, Alex Stonehill suggests that violent conflicts over water are inevitable. Stonehill tells the story of ethnic Somali herders relegated to Ethiopian refugee camps after losing a war over water. Stonehill says fights between farmers and herders over water are common and contributed to the genocides in Darfur and Rwanda. Stonehill also tells about conflicts arising over the lack of basic water infrastructure in East African slums. Stonehill believes that many of Earth's lakes and rivers will eventually dry up from overuse and climate change impacts. Once this happens, and millions of people from many different countries are left competing for scant water supplies, armed conflicts will be inevitable, says Stonehill. Stonehill is a

Alex Stonehill, "World Water Crisis," *Z Magazine*, June 19, 2008. Copyright © 2008 Alex Stonehill. Reproduced by permission of the author. www.zmag.org.

Seattle-based journalist and cofounder of the nonprofit Common Language Project, which is devoted to humane international journalism.

As you read, consider the following questions:

1. At the Refugee camp outside the Muslim city of Harar, Stonehill describes people who lost all of their livestock and many of their family members. How are these people currently getting water to drink and wash, according to Stonehill?

2. According to Stonehill, in Nairobi, the city water infrastructure ends at the edge of Kibera, the second largest slum in the African continent. How do the people of Kibera get their water?

3. According to Stonehill, which countries share the water resources of the Lake Victoria/Nile River system?

Water is the new oil. While western politicians and consumers fret over the declining economy and increasing oil prices, the news from East Africa is that with a growing majority of the world living on less than a dollar a day, the liquid that fuels bodies is becoming even more contentious than the liquid that fuels cars.

I've spent the last four months reporting stories about water from Ethiopia and Kenya, two countries at the forefront of the world's coming water crisis. The director of a local water NGO [nongovernmental organization] told me a few days after I arrived in Ethiopia in January 2008, "As you may know, Alex, the coming World War III will be fought over water, not oil." Variations on that refrain were echoed by aid workers and researchers across the region over the next several months. Women walk for miles each day to collect drinking water; farmers are pushed into deadly conflict by dwindling river flows, and city water supplies are drained by overzealous irrigation. The bigger picture that the smaller stories hint at is one of ecological disaster and conflict over resources that will affect millions and have repercussions around the world.

Water War Refugees

The fringes of Ethiopia's fertile highlands are dotted with camps housing refugees from water-based conflicts in the rest of the country. A few kilometers outside the ancient Muslim city of Harar, alongside a dry river bed, lies one such camp of 5,000 ethnic Somalis. They were driven from the Ogaden region by inter-clan conflict over access to water and pastureland. The camp is a sprawling expanse of small, wood-framed domes covered with a patchwork of plastic and other scrap material, whatever families can scavenge to shield themselves from the equatorial sun.

These people lost all their livestock, as well as many of their family members, to the conflict, and they now survive on cactus and occasional handouts from the locals. In recent months that hospitality has begun to wear thin as well. To get water to drink and wash they dig into the sandy bottom of the dry riverbed until they've scratched deep enough to reveal the muddy water that flows beneath.

The elders of the village earnestly described their situation to me, asking hopefully if I knew anyone who could help, but I suspected that their story would never find its way into the media. After all, the scale of their tragedy can't compare to other African conflicts that are making the news and there isn't any element of geopolitical intrigue here—just poor people fighting over water.

I later realized that, in fact, the scale of this story was massive. Refugees from similar conflicts over access to shrinking water and pastureland are scattered across southern Ethiopia and northern Kenya.

The Struggle for Freshwater

Given the difficulties of sensibly apportioning the water supply within a single nation, imagine the complexities of doing so for international river basins such as that of the Jordan River, which borders on Lebanon, Syria, Israel, the Palestinian areas and Jordan, all of which have claims to the shared, but limited, supply in an extremely parched region. The struggle for freshwater has contributed to civil and military disputes in the area. Only continuing negotiations and compromise have kept this tense situation under control.

Peter Rogers, "Facing the Freshwater Crisis,"
Scientific American, *August 2008.*

Herders Fight over Water for Their Animals

Pastoralists [those who depend on livestock for their livelihood] are especially vulnerable to climate change because they already live so close to the margins, dependant on grazing their cattle and camels in areas where agriculture is barely viable. A small decrease in rainfall can be a death sentence for animals if sparse watering holes go dry. Most herders are armed against predators and would sooner clash with other groups to get access to water than stand by and watch their animals die.

The two main insurgencies currently beleaguering the Ethiopian government are devoted to the independence of Oromia and the Ogaden, both long-neglected lowland areas with large pastoralist populations. Neighboring Somalia, which for over 15 years has been dominated by inter-clan conflicts like the one that displaced the refugees in Ethiopia, is an extension of the same arid lowland and is almost entirely populated by pastoralists as well. Even the genocides in Darfur and Rwanda were born from the cultural collisions between pastoralists and farmers.

There's no denying that these are politically motivated conflicts, but the role water scarcity plays in creating the preconditions of desperation and discontent is equally undeniable.

City Dwellers Fight over Water Inequities

"Water is life" is a phrase repeated over and over again by East African aid workers. But a more revealing variation might be "water symbolizes wealth." Even in highland urban capitals like Addis Ababa and Nairobi, where temperatures are cool and rains are plentiful, access to clean drinking water and sanitation facilities tops the list of problems cited by slum dwellers, who make up half the population of some cities. Deaths from waterborne disease usually receive less attention, although they typically exceed deaths from AIDS.

In Nairobi city water infrastructure ends at the edge of Kibera, the continent's second largest slum. An informal private sector of water vendors takes over from there, jerry-rigging a network of cheap plastic pipes and water tanks that taint the water with free flowing sewage. The million people who live in Kibera typically end up paying hundreds of times more than those in other Nairobi neighborhoods for water that makes them sick.

Slum residents are angry about this kind of government neglect. Tensions increase further when such neglect appears to exist along ethnic lines. When slum residents riot, as they did following last December's elections in Kenya, it is usually presented in the media as violence in a vacuum or as ethnic strife. But it's no coincidence that this kind of violence often breaks out in places where people lack access to basic services like water and don't have many other options for getting the attention of their political leaders. When chaos erupted in

Kibera in January, some of the first targets for vandalism were tanks owned by water vendors who had been price gouging for years.

Water Resources Drying Up

A Ugandan environmentalist told me about the nightmare prospect of the world's second largest lake drying up completely. Lake Victoria's levels have receded by several meters in recent years, destroying the breeding grounds for fish, and endangering the 30 million East Africans who live around the lake. Kenyans chasing fish into deeper Ugandan waters have been arrested and allegedly tortured by Ugandan military.

In addition to rising temperatures, decreased rainfall, and watershed deforestation, scientists and fisher-people alike blame new hydroelectric projects at the source of the River Nile in Uganda from draining too much water out of the shrinking lake.

Without international cooperation on conservation, this sort of tit for tat race to exploit resources faster than a neighbor may ensure that Lake Victoria ends up like other devastated bodies of water, such as the Aral Sea and Lake Chad.

Conflicts over the water resources of the Lake Victoria/ Nile River system seem almost inevitable. The nine countries that share the system (Egypt, Ethiopia, Sudan, Tanzania, Kenya, Uganda, Burundi, Rwanda, and the Democratic Republic of Congo) are some of the world's poorest nations and their populations are exploding, increasing stress on endangered water resources.

Just as Kenyan farmers are decreasing inflows into Lake Victoria by cutting forests in its watersheds, the Ugandan government is increasing outflows by running more water through its new dams into the Nile. Just as Ethiopians are pushing to industrialize their agricultural sector for export, putting new land under irrigation, hundreds of miles down-river Egypt is channeling millions of gallons of water out of the river to "reclaim" vast swaths of desert.

With the current regional population of 387 million on course to double in the next 30 years, the equation of available gallons of water from this system just doesn't add up. Movements for international cooperation, such as the Nile Basin Initiative, have yielded some promising results, but in a corner of the world already fraught with tense rivalries, control over the most basic human resource is almost certain to be a cause for violent conflict.

Water Wars a Reminder That Natural Resources Intertwined with Human Prosperity

For Americans, environmentalism has traditionally been concerned with preserving natural beauty for its own sake and protecting nature from the advances of civilization. But in East Africa, home to an impressive environmental movement, environmentalism is inseparable from humanitarianism. Here, when ecosystems are destroyed, people are almost always directly harmed as well, even if they are the ones doing the destroying.

The experiences of Africans struggling to find fish in Lake Victoria or fighting over dwindling pastureland for their livestock in Ethiopia might not seem like particularly important stories for U.S. news audiences. But these small stories are relevant for what they tell us about the story of the planet as an ecological whole. When violence over access to basic resources like water erupts among people who depend directly on the earth for their survival, it is an important reminder. Despite the distinctions we've imagined between the survival of the natural environment and our own prosperity, the health of the earth and the health of humans are one and the same.

| "In fact, when two countries share water resources, this may lead to increased cooperation—rather than increased conflict."

Armed Conflicts Will Not Arise over Water Scarcity

Andrew Biro

In the following viewpoint, Andrew Biro asserts that armed conflicts on a large scale will not result from water scarcity. He doesn't find any evidence to support the idea that such conflicts would arise. Biro thinks worries about water wars are just a sign of the times—more a reflection of our cultural environment than a bona fide reason for worry. Biro thinks it's more likely that countries will share water resources than fight over them. He does believe that conflicts over water will arise. There will, however, be low-intensity, subnational conflicts between the "haves" and the "have-nots." Biro holds a Canada Research Chair in political ecology and is an assistant professor in the Department of Political Science at Acadia University in Nova Scotia.

As you read, consider the following questions:

1. According to Biro, the prospect of "water wars" fits with the view that globalization is the cause of chaos and anarchy. Name the three contemporary anxieties, which Biro also says fit with this view of globalization.

2. According to Biro, only one unambiguous example of an armed conflict occurred over water. When and where did this conflict occur?

3. According to Biro, virtually all of the projected growth in the world's population will occur where?

What a difference a few years make. In the mid-1990s, Ismail Serageldin, then the World Bank's Vice President for Environmentally and Socially Sustainable Development, declared, "If the wars of this [20th] century were fought over oil, the wars of the next century will be fought over water."

In contrast, in the Brundtland Commission's seminal 1987 report, *Our Common Future*, water use issues on a global scale were a relatively minor concern, warranting only one paragraph out of the report's nearly 400 pages.

Are Water War Worries *Really* About Water?

How is it possible that something that should be obvious— looming scarcity of one of the most essential materials for human life—could arise so suddenly?

Partly, this increased anxiety over the prospect of "water wars" reflects our current ecological reality: Over the past century, global water use has risen steadily, driven upwards in roughly equal measures by population growth and economic development. But neither of these trends was unknown to people in the 1970s and 1980s.

Another part of the explanation for the current anxiety lies in our cultural environment. The prospect of "water wars" fits well with contemporary popular narratives. In water wars, we assume that we would see the brutal side of human nature emerging as we come face-to-face with scarcity.

The *Survivor* reality TV franchise provides a popular example of this kind of narrative, even if in that case both the scarcity and the conflict are engineered for viewers' presumed entertainment.

The prospect of "water wars" also fits with the view that global interconnections foster a "coming anarchy," arriving at our doors from other parts of the globe. The view that chaos is being brought home by the forces of globalization resonates with all sorts of contemporary anxieties, from terrorism to the global spread of diseases like SARS [Severe Acute Respiratory Syndrome] and on to the prospect of massive migration forced by environmental changes ("climate refugees").

So is a future of "water wars" all but inevitable, or is this nothing more than environmental scare-mongering? Just to pose the question in this way misses a third possibility—that we are already living in a world where access to water is determined, borrowing geographer Michael Watts' description of famine, by "silent violence."

Global Water Supply: The Issue Is Circulation

While difficult to measure precisely, by most accounts, the world's water supply is well over a billion cubic kilometers. On the other hand, total surface freshwater—the water we can actually use—is estimated to be less than 100,000 cubic kilometers—a miniscule fraction of the world's total water supply.

But global water supply is not all that relevant, since water is a renewable resource. Water gets moved around and stored in various forms: Not just lakes and oceans, but also ice caps, clouds, underground aquifers and even in living beings (Star Trek fans may remember the description of humans as "ugly bags of mostly water").

The point is that it never disappears completely. Even the ratio of fresh to salt water is fairly stable. (Climate change has an impact on this, but rising sea levels—more salt water—may to some extent be counterbalanced by higher evaporation rates and thus more frequent precipitation).

The issue is: How quickly does it circulate—or how much of our accessible supply of fresh water is replenished over a given period of time?

In 1992, Sandra Postel, one of the first to warn of global water scarcity, estimated that the global "relatively stable source of supply"—rainfall onto land that does not run off in large floods—is about 14,000 cubic kilometers annually.

Estimates of total human water use, like estimates of water supply, vary quite a lot. Most estimates are somewhere in the vicinity of 5,000 cubic kilometers per year.

In other words, we are currently using about one-third of the water supplies effectively available to us. This might seem like a substantial cushion, but both population growth and economic development are continuing to cut into it.

With our global population projected to peak at 50% higher than its current level, and economic development a largely unquestioned imperative in rich as well as poor countries, water scarcity in the future looks like a greater possibility.

Water Is Local

Looking at the global water picture, like looking at total volume rather than renewal rate, may also be a case of trying to measure the wrong thing. We need water at specific places and times.

And in most cases, our water is much more likely to be locally sourced than the vehicles we drive, the music we listen to and the food we eat.

This is true for a number of reasons. First, water is a fluid but dense substance. One cubic meter, or 1,000 liters, of water

Water Can Create Peace, Not War

Simply put, water as a greater pathway to peace than conflict in the world's international river basins. International cooperation around water has a long and successful history; some of the world's most vociferous enemies have negotiated water agreements. The institutions they have created are resilient, even when relations are strained. The Mekong Committee, for example, established by Cambodia, Laos, Thailand, and Vietnam in 1957, exchanged data and information on the river basin throughout the Vietnam War.

Israel and Jordan held secret "picnic table" talks to manage the Jordan River starting in 1953, even though they were officially at war from 1948 until the 1994 treaty.

Aaron Wolf, Annika Kramer,
Alexander Carius, and Geoffrey Dabelko,
"Water Can Be a Pathway to Peace, Not War,"
July 2006. http://wilsoncenter.org.

has a mass of one ton—so a substantial amount of energy is required to get it to do anything other than flow downhill.

Second, we require large amounts on a daily basis: About 50 liters—50 kilograms—is a frequently cited figure for the daily per capita minimum required for basic drinking, cooking, cleaning and sanitation.

Third, in spite of its vital importance, its economic value in most uses is relatively low. Water values are often measured in mere cents per cubic meter.

Taken together, these make the transportation of large amounts of water across significant distances sensible only under exceptional circumstances. And "water wars," if they occur, are likely to be quite localized. . . .

History Provides Few Examples of Water Wars

Because both human populations and freshwater are unevenly distributed around the world, some locales are likely to be affected by serious water scarcity problems long before global withdrawals reach the level of global sustainable supplies. If this is the case, shouldn't we be seeing water wars already?

According to Aaron Wolf of the University of Oregon, a prominent geographer who has conducted extensive studies of conflict and cooperation in shared river basins, history provides very few examples of "water wars" in the sense of armed conflict between states over water resources.

In fact, Wolf found only one unambiguous example—and that was between two city-states in the Tigris-Euphrates valley 4,500 years ago. In fact, when two countries share water resources, this may lead to increased cooperation—rather than increased conflict.

Another reason for the lack of water wars has to do with the fact that domestic or household use accounts for only about 10% of total water consumption. The rest is used to produce other things, predominantly agricultural goods.

So rather than importing large volumes of water (much less fighting wars over it), water shortages may more often be managed by diverting water to households, reducing the amount provided for things like irrigation, and then importing water-intensive goods rather than producing them locally.

Low-Intensity, Sub-National Conflicts

According to Wolf, even if there are very few water wars between countries, "there is a history of water-related violence—it is a history of incidents at the sub-national level, generally between ethnic, religious or tribal groups, water-use sector, or states/provinces."

California's "water wars" of the early 20th century (an episode brilliantly fictionalized in Roman Polanski's 1974 film noir *Chinatown*) provide an example of this sort of low-intensity, sub-national conflict.

Who decides how water scarcity is to be managed? In Southern California, small farmers were squeezed out by urban development interests, playing on popular fears of water scarcity that were partly grounded in ecological realities—but also partly invented.

Water Losers Migrating to Cities Creating Proliferation of Slums in Southern Hemisphere

A shift in how a country's water supply is divided among water users—with less for farmers (whose products can be replaced with imported goods), and more for urban residents—is necessarily a political process, with winners and losers.

Small farmers, with little political or economic clout, are frequently among the losers, and as a result often eventually have no choice but to migrate to cities. Southern California's history a century ago is being replayed all over the world today, as small farmers are unable to compete in food markets that have been opened up to global competition.

As agriculture is increasingly globalized and industrialized, we are becoming an increasingly urban species. The global human population just passed the 50% urban mark. Virtually all of the projected growth in the world's population—another three billion or so people before the population levels off later this century—will occur in the cities of the Global South.

Unlike in the past, this contemporary phase of urbanization is largely occurring without economic growth, and largely in places where governments have the least capacity to manage human migration and urban development.

The result has been an astonishing proliferation of slums in cities throughout the Global South. And it is in these dense concentrations of urban poverty that we find many of the people who struggle daily to get enough water.

The technology to deliver clean water to densely concentrated populations is not new. And with a few exceptions, most cities have adequate water supplies relatively close at hand. The real challenge is neither technological nor ecological, but political and economic.

To put it another way, a lack of access to adequate clean water supplies has very little to do with water scarcity caused by drought or overuse, and has much more to do with a lack of investment in the basic infrastructure required to treat and deliver water to people.

In the developed world, governments from the 19th century onward spent large amounts of money building urban water infrastructure, solving public health problems and providing citizens with a tangible benefit of citizenship. For a variety of reasons, the networks of pipes and taps that most in the developed world can now take for granted have not materialized for new urban populations. . . .

Water Wars Are Really Class Wars

As it stands, the forces of economic globalization have acted like a giant set of pincers on the poor of the Global South. On the one hand, untold millions are migrating to cities, due— among other reasons—to the globalization of agricultural trade.

On the other hand, governments are being deprived of the capacity to make critical investments in the infrastructure necessary to sustain booming urban populations.

For some, water is effectively granted as a right, provided at low cost by the state. For many others—usually those who can least afford it—it is treated as a commodity that must be bought. Access to water is in fact much more closely tied to social class than to climate. In this sense, the conflicts arising from water scarcity are class wars.

> *"Conservation and recycling alone won't be enough, but combined with seawater desalination, California has a real solution."*

Desalination Is an Important Part of the Solution to California's Water Crisis

Peter MacLaggan

In the following viewpoint, Peter MacLaggan contends that the time has come for desalination projects—in which salt is removed from seawater—to be considered a key part of the solution to the world's, and particularly California's, water crisis. MacLaggan is responding to an opinion piece published in the "Dust-Up" section of the Los Angeles Times, *in which conservationist Mindy McIntyre voiced her opposition to a desalination project in Carlsbad, California, saying "desalination is impractical." MacLaggan says this is outdated thinking. He says desalination technologies have advanced to the point where they are practical and are competitive with any new water-producing technology. According to MacLaggan, it's unfortunate that McIntyre and others have slowed down the Carlsbad project, because desalination can help solve California's water crisis. MacLaggan is senior vice president of Poseidon Resources Corporation, a company that specializes in developing desalination projects.*

As you read, consider the following questions:

1. According to MacLaggan, how many desalination plants are there in the world and how much drinking water do they produce in a day?

2. According to MacLaggan, California's water supply system is based on what?

3. According to MacLaggan, the Carlsbad desalination project will be the first major infrastructure project in California to do what?

Mindy McIntyre of the Planning and Conservation League opines in an installment of "Dust-Up" [a section of the *Los Angeles Times*], "The SUV of water," that seawater desalination is impractical. It's 2008; innovation, technology and an evolving regulatory and environmental landscape render McIntyre's Model T-era assertion incredible and outdated.

Today, there are more than 21,000 desalination plants in 120 countries around the world producing 3 billion gallons of drinking water a day. Rest assured the world does not know something that we don't—California has a dozen plants in various stages of permitting, including a 50-million-gallon-a-day plant in Carlsbad that will be the largest and most technologically advanced in the Western Hemisphere. Local, state and federal policy makers and water resource managers are aggressively pursuing seawater desalination in an effort to diversify water portfolios and protect against drought-inflicted blows to the economy and public health. Still, not everyone is honestly confronting the reality that new potable water supplies are not unlimited, choosing instead to believe that we can simply conserve our way out of the next water supply crisis.

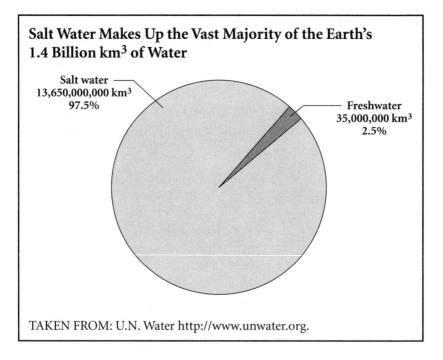

Salt Water Makes Up the Vast Majority of the Earth's 1.4 Billion km³ of Water

Salt water
13,650,000,000 km³
97.5%

Freshwater
35,000,000 km³
2.5%

TAKEN FROM: U.N. Water http://www.unwater.org.

California's water supply system is based largely on pumping water from environmentally sensitive watersheds in Northern California and the Colorado River over hundreds of miles to Southern California through an elaborate and costly network of dams, canals and reservoirs. But proven desalination technology now allows us to produce higher-quality water along the coast, where the majority of the state's population resides, at a comparable cost and without damaging the environmentally sensitive upstream habitats.

It is true that seawater desalination historically has been prohibitively expensive, but today this is no longer the case due in large part to technological advances and the escalating cost and scarcity of traditional water sources. Yes, energy is one of the cost variables associated with the production of desalinated water; however, the same is true for the transportation of imported water and the treatment of reclaimed water. In truth, the escalating energy costs that McIntyre worries about—and associates only with seawater desalination—will affect all means of new drinking water production.

More than just a new water supply project, the Carlsbad desalination [project] will be the first major infrastructure project in the state to eliminate its carbon footprint. This voluntary commitment is unprecedented, and it has led many to believe that the project will help set the tone for the implementation of AB [Assembly Bill] 32, California's groundbreaking Global Warming Solutions Act.[1]

The bigger concern facing Californians is the inordinate time it takes to build infrastructure that addresses a dire public need. The Carlsbad facility was introduced a decade ago [1993], and has spent the last five years [2003–2008] winding its way through the state's permitting process. Every regulatory agency, including the heavyweight environmental watchdog California Coastal Commission and the State Water Quality Control Board, have determined that the project is necessary and can be built and operated without negatively affecting the environment. McIntyre, and a few unsatisfied others, have opposed this project every step of the way, filing appeals and lawsuits to slow down a potable water project that will provide a drought-proof supply to 300,000 Californians.

To put this challenge into proper perspective, during the same period that the Carlsbad desalination project has been navigating the California regulatory process, Australia, in response to severe drought conditions similar to those we are experiencing here in the Southwest, has commissioned one major desalination facility in Perth, has two projects under construction and three more projects in various stages of planning that are expected to be operational by 2011. The combined capacity of these facilities is 180 million gallons a day.

1. Signed into law September 27, 2006, the Global Warming Solutions Act established a comprehensive set of regulatory and market mechanisms to measurably reduce greenhouse gases.

Seawater desalination is not a silver bullet that will allow California to single-handedly avoid a water supply crisis, but it is a critical part of the effort at all levels of government to diversify the state's water supply portfolio. The general public, elected officials and water resource managers overwhelmingly support seawater desalination because its time has come. Conservation and recycling alone won't be enough, but combined with seawater desalination, California has a real solution.

"Those who look to desalination as the future panacea to the world's water problems may be glossing over considerable environmental, economic and social difficulties."

Desalination Should Not Play a Major Role in Helping to Solve Water Problems

Phil Dickie

In the following viewpoint, Phil Dickie of the World Wildlife Fund (WWF) contends that desalination projects should play only a limited role in addressing the world's water problems. According to the WWF, not enough attention is being paid to the fact that desalination is very costly, emits pollutants, can degrade marine habitats, and can exacerbate global warming. The WWF notes that the high costs of building and operating desalination plants makes it unlikely they will be used to help poor people in developing countries. The author maintains that desalination may have a limited place in providing new sources of water, but

Phil Dickie, Melaleuca Media Pty Ltd for WWF International, *Making Water: Desalination—Option or Distraction for a Thirsty World?* Gland, Switzerland: World Wildlife Fund, 2007. Copyright © 2007 WWF (panda.org). Reproduced by permission.

all of its environmental, social, and economic issues must be considered first. The World Wildlife Fund is one of the largest conservation organizations in the world.

As you read, consider the following questions:

1. According to the World Wildlife Fund (WWF), where does desalination make the greatest contribution to urban water supplies?

2. The WWF is worried about desalination having the potential to drive a misdirection of public policy away from what?

3. The WWF's view of desalination is that it needs to be considered on a case-by-case basis in line with integrated approaches to the management of water supply and demand. According to the WWF, central to this approach is the protection of what?

A s the world increasingly comes to the realisation that a combination of population increases, development demands and climate change means that freshwater will be in chronically short supply in rich and poor areas of the world alike, there is increasing interest in desalination as a technique for tapping into the vast and infinitely tempting water supplies of the sea.

This is no new dream, and it has been technically possible to separate the salt and the water for centuries. But widespread desalination for the purpose of general water supply for land-based communities has been limited by its great expense and it is notable that the area where desalination currently makes by far the greatest contribution to urban water supplies is in the oil-rich and water poor States around the Persian Gulf.

More Countries Looking at Desalination, but Glossing over Difficulties

Now, however, improvements in the technology of desalination, coupled with the rising cost and increasing unreliability of traditional water supplies, are bringing desalinated water into more focus as a general water supply option with major plants in operation, in planning or under consideration in Europe, North Africa, North America, Australia, China and India among others.

In 2004, it was estimated that seawater desalination capacity would increase 101 per percent by 2015, an addition of an additional 31 million m3 [cubic meters] a day. The dominant membrane based technologies would also be used extensively in desalinating brackish waters and recycling water generally. But these forecasts, regarded as bold at the time, seem certain to be exceeded by wide margins. In one example, the forecast was for China and India to be desalinating 650,000 m3 a day by 2015, but China alone has recently announced plans to be desalinating 1 million m3 of seawater a day by 2010 increasing to 3 million m3 a day by 2020.

But those who look to desalination as the future panacea to the world's water problems may be glossing over considerable environmental, economic and social difficulties. Despite improved technologies and reduced costs, desalinated water remains highly expensive and sensitive in particular to increases in energy costs. Our knowledge of impacts is largely based on limited research from relatively small plants operating in relative isolation from each other. The future being indicated by public water authorities and the desalination industry is of ever larger plants that will frequently be clustered together in the relatively sensitive coastal environments that most attract extensive settlement.

The difficulties are both direct and indirect, but they warrant closer attention than they seem to be receiving from

© Ralph Hagen/www.CartoonStock.com.

some of the desalination industry's most enthusiastic proponents and some of the regulatory bodies currently considering large scale desalination.

Cost, Pollution, and Energy Consumption Must Be Considered

Direct problems include the still significant problem of cost, the pollution emitted by desalination plants and the energy they consume. Seawater, it has been pointed out, is also habitat. The larvae and small organisms most vulnerable to disappearing up a poorly designed desalination plant inlet pipe play key roles in marine ecosystems. And our knowledge of the impacts and behaviours of the concentrated brines and diverse other chemicals issuing from the outlet pipe is far from comprehensive, both generally and in relation to particular sites.

There are also serious greenhouse gas emission implications in driving the energy intensive plants, which could thereby contribute a key driving factor behind the looming chronic water shortages in many of the areas where desalination is being actively considered.

Less directly, the quite possibly mistaken lure of widespread water availability from desalination also has the potential to drive a major misdirection of public attention, policy and funds away from the pressing need to use all water wisely. Desalination in these terms is firmly in the long established tradition of large infrastructure supply side solutions to an issue in which the demand side of the equation is usually poorly considered—as are the needs of the environment and the people who might be in the way.

There is also the question of equity to consider. Desalination through its cost and technical requirements is likely to be mainly used in addressing the water worries of the already wealthy. There are few indications that a growing desalination industry left to its own devices will pay much attention to the more pressing water needs of the many people in developing nations living in arid areas with brackish or contaminated groundwater supplies. This may be an issue of particular importance to the many millions living in areas of developed countries where overdrawing of groundwaters has allowed the oxidation and mobilisation of dangerous soil elements such as arsenic and fluorides. The reverse osmosis membrane technologies used increasingly in desalination have been used successfully in a limited way in parts of India to remove dangerous contaminants from rural drinking water—there are clear humanitarian reasons to deploy the technology much more widely.

Reverse osmosis membrane technologies have great potential for increasing water use efficiency through recycling, for decontaminating water and for environmental repair through purifying or providing water for such purposes as rejuvenating wetlands, augmenting streamflows and recharging aquifers. Manufacturing or recycling water can also relieve the pressure on overstressed natural water sources, allowing them the opportunity for recovery. Indeed as the economic and energy costs of manufacturing water are closely related to the level of contaminants, desalination of seawater is commonly more expensive than desalination of brackish water or treatment and recycling of waste water.

Desalination Has a Limited Place

The considered view of WWF is that seawater desalination has a limited place in water supply, which needs to be considered on a case by case basis in line with integrated approaches to the management of water supply and demand. Central to such an approach is the protection of the natural assets of catchments, rivers, floodplains, lakes, wetlands, aquifers and vapour flows which ultimately provide, store, supply, and purify water and provide the best and most comprehensive protection against extreme or catastrophic events.

To that end, WWF proposes an approach similar to that recommended for large dams by the World Commission on Dams that says that proponents should first assess the need and then consider all options to select the best solution. Desalination plants, accordingly, should only be constructed where they are found to meet a genuine need to increase water supply and are the best and least damaging method of augmenting water supply, after a process which is open, exhaustive, and fully transparent and in which all alternatives, especially demand side and pollution control measures, are properly considered and fairly costed in their environmental, economic and social impacts.

WWF is calling on governments, financing agencies and relevant areas and peak bodies of the water industry to work to endorse and help develop specific protocols that start from these premises. We also note that we are not alone in this. The prestigious Pacific Institute made recommendations to this general effect in relation to California and similar comments have been made to the industry by a senior World Bank official.

Periodical Bibliography

Adam Bluestein   "Blue Is the New Green," *Inc*, November 2008.

Mark Clayton   "Is Water Becoming the New Oil?" *Christian Science Monitor*, May 29, 2008.

Kevin Ferguson   "Water Mismanagement Plagues the World's Poor," *Business Week Online*, March 26, 2009.

Jeneen Interl   "Rivers Running Dry," *Newsweek*, April 28, 2008.

Brook Larmer   "Bitter Waters: A Crisis Is Brewing in China's Northern Heartland as Its Lifeline, the Yellow River, Succumbs to Pollution and Overuse," *National Geographic*, May 2008.

Ryan Leaderman and   "Commentary: California Water Worries: Big
Linda Bozung   Solutions Are Needed to Head Off a Serious Water Crisis," *Our Planet*, February 3, 2009.

Eric D. Mintz and   "A Lion in Our Village—The Unconscionable
Richard L. Guerrant   Tragedy of Cholera in Africa," *New England Journal of Medicine*, March 12, 2009.

Roy Roberson   "Southeast Faces Water Management Crisis," *Southeast Farm Press*, August 11, 2008.

Thom Senzee   "Drought May Be Over, but Water Crisis Still Very Real: Decades of Inertia, Environmental Concerns Contribute," *San Fernando Valley Business Journal*, March 3, 2008.

Paul Sinclair   "An Unholy Water Crisis: What Can Australia Learn About Water Management from Israel?" *Habitat Australia*, April 2008.

Western Farm Press   "California Water Crisis Battle Continues to Erupt on Many Fronts," February 21, 2009.

David Zetland   "The Water Shortage Myth," *Forbes*, July 14, 2008. www.forbes.com.

How Should Water Resources Be Managed?

Chapter Preface

At the 2005 annual Agriculture and Natural Resources (ANR) week gathering at Michigan State University, a gentleman from Illinois gave an impassioned plea. He said he loved the Great Lakes dearly and was deeply troubled by the grave threat facing the Lakes from invasive species. He was particularly worried about Asian carp from the Mississippi River entering the Great Lakes via the Chicago Sanitary and Ship Canal. He pleaded with the scientists, government officials, and policy makers who were in attendance at the meeting to do whatever they could to stop the Asian carp from getting through the canal. The man from Illinois is not alone. Many scientists and lovers of the Great Lakes are deeply troubled by the threat of the Asian carp. In response, the U.S. Army Corps of Engineers has been building an electric barrier in the Chicago Sanitary and Ship Canal to prevent the Asian carp from entering Lake Michigan and other Great Lakes' waters.

The Asian carp entered the Mississippi River after flooding many years ago. Back in the 1970s, catfish farmers from Arkansas and other southern states imported two species of Asian carp—bighead carp and silver carp—to eat algae and suspended matter from their catfish ponds. The farmers made a good selection when they chose Asian carp. The fish are ravenous eaters. A single twenty-five-pound carp typically eats ten or more pounds of plankton daily. The carp did a good job keeping the Southern catfish ponds clean for more than twenty years. Major flooding during the early 1990s, however, caused many of the catfish ponds to overflow and release the carp into local waterways—waterways connected to the Mississippi River.

Once they entered the Mississippi, the carp made their presence known as they moved north up the river. In addition to being ravenous eaters, the bighead carp and the silver carp reproduce rapidly. It did not take much time for hundreds of thousands of the fish—most weighing twenty-five pounds, but some reaching weights of eighty to one hundred pounds—to start competing with native fish and to take over the river, moving northward the whole time. The carp also became notorious for leaping into boats and even injuring boaters, water skiers, and jet skiers. Ruth Nissen from the Wisconsin Department of Natural Resources says, "Imagine if you can, 10–20 pound fish jumping into your boat as you idle in a side channel of the Mississippi River. A classic fish story, but one that has become true in the Missouri and Mississippi Rivers. In reality, it is a situation than can be downright hazardous especially when a 20-pound fish comes flying at your head."

Eventually, the Asian carp made its way to the Illinois River and started causing concern for the Great Lakes ecosystem. The Illinois River is connected to Lake Michigan via the Chicago Sanitary and Ship Canal. The canal is artificial. It was erected in the late 1800s to allow Chicago to send wastewater down the Illinois and Mississippi river systems rather than pollute Lake Michigan—its water source. The canal now provides a shipping route between the Great Lakes and the Mississippi. It also provides a conduit between the Mississippi River ecosystem and the Great Lakes ecosystem—a conduit that can be traversed by Asian carp and other invasive species. According to the Great Lakes Fisheries Commission, "The carp are in the canal and have been sighted approximately 40 miles from Lake Michigan."

Asian carp pose a significant threat to the entire Great Lakes ecosystem. Asian carp are well-suited to the cold water climate of the Great Lakes region, which is similar to their native Eastern Hemisphere habitats. It is expected that if they get to the Great Lakes, the carp would compete for food with the sport and commercial fish of the Great Lakes—and the carp would win. The fear is that they would eradicate trout, salmon, walleye, white fish, and other Great Lakes' fish and completely change the entire Great Lakes ecosystem. According to Joel Brammeier, from the Alliance for the Great Lakes, "Invaders like Asian carp are unpredictable, but their effects are catastrophic and irreversible. Every day we allow them closer to the Great Lakes, the threat grows larger."

To prevent the carp from entering the Great Lakes, the U.S. Army Corps of Engineers constructed an electric barrier across the Chicago Sanitary and Ship Canal at a site in a heavily industrialized corner of the city. A series of cables strung across the bottom of the canal near Romeoville, Illinois, send out steady pulses of electricity, strong enough to repel a fish, but not hurt or kill it. The idea is that as fish pass through the barrier, they feel increasing levels of electricity, which prompts them to turn around. An experimental electric barrier, which sent out one volt of electricity, began operating in 2002. The permanent barrier, erected several years later (2009), sends out four volts of electricity. The electric barrier is the main line of defense the government has put in place to keep the Asian carp out of the Great Lakes.

The barrier has seen some controversy—the permanent barrier has taken longer than expected to build and barge operators are concerned about its safety—but many people are hoping the barrier can keep the Asian carp out of the Great Lakes, at least for the short term. Some experts say that to permanently and completely protect the Great Lakes from Asian carp would likely require reengineering Chicago-area waterways to once again separate the waters of the Great Lakes from the Mississippi River. The electric carp barrier is just one example of many illustrating how, throughout history, humans have changed the course of rivers; constructed artificial dams, lakes, and reservoirs; and established laws and policies to protect and control water resources. In the following chapter, the contributors debate various other water resource management issues.

> *"Most of the water that will sustain the expected 15 million additional Californians is going to come from agriculture. It has to."*

Transferring Water from Agricultural to Urban Use Is Beneficial

Robert Glennon

In the following viewpoint, Robert Glennon believes that the United States is heading toward a crisis in water supply and has limited options to address it. He believes one very important option is to create water markets that facilitate the transfer of agricultural water to fast-growing urban areas. Farmers, particularly those in western states, have powerful rights to water that were provided to them under the federal Reclamation Act of 1902. Glennon says that farmers use millions of gallons of water, wasting much of it in the process, to irrigate marginal lands that produce low-value crops. If, under government oversight, farmers were able to sell their water to parched cities, it would help satisfy the cities' huge water demands and create incentives for farmers to better manage water. Furthermore, it could help put

Robert Glennon, "Water Scarcity, Marketing, and Privatization," *Texas Law Review*, vol. 83, June 2005, pp. 1873–74, 1876, 1878–89, 1902. Copyright © 2005 Texas Law Review. Reproduced by permission. http://papers.ssrn.com.

money in the pockets of struggling farmers. Glennon believes moving water from agricultural to urban use, or water realloca- tion, is a win-win situation. Glennon is the Morris K. Udall professor of law and public policy at the University of Arizona's (UA's) Rogers College of Law and a member of the UA Water Resources Research Center.

As you read, consider the following questions:

1. According to Glennon, how many American rivers are free flowing?

2. What is Glennon's third option for satisfying new water demands?

3. According to Glennon, irrigation systems, which consist of primitive earthen canals, lose what percentage of the water diverted into them? Where does the water go?

4. According to Glennon, what is the core idea of markets?

Most Americans take water for granted. Turn on the tap and a limitless quantity of high quality water flows for less money than it costs for cable television or a cell phone. The current [2005] drought has raised awareness of water scarcity, but most proposals for dealing with drought involve quick fixes—short-term palliatives, such as bans on washing cars or watering lawns except on alternate days. It is assumed that things will return to normal, and we will be able to wash our cars whenever we wish. But the nation's water supply is not inexhaustible. A just-released report of a White House subcommittee ominously begins: "Does the United States have enough water? We do not know." In a survey of states con- ducted by the U.S. General Accounting Office, only 14 states reported that they did not expect to suffer water shortages in the next 10 years.

Is the sky falling? Not yet, but the United States is heading toward a water scarcity crisis: our current water use practices are unsustainable, and environmental factors threaten a water supply heavily burdened by increased demand. As the demand for water outstrips the supply, the stage is set for what [evolutionary biologist] Jared Diamond would call a collapse. How will we respond? When we needed more water in the past, we built a dam, dug a canal, or drilled a well. With some exceptions, these options are no longer viable due to a paucity of sites, dwindling supplies, escalating costs, and environmental objections. Instead, we are entering an era in which demand for new water will be satisfied by reallocating and conserving existing sources. The current water rights structure is the outcome of historical forces that conferred great wealth and power along with the water. The solution to tomorrow's water shortages will require creative answers to challenging issues of equity, community, and economics. . . .

Limited Options to Satisfy Increasing Water Demands

As the nation's water use spirals upward, where will the water come from to satisfy new demands? We have five options. First, we could simply continue to exploit the resource by diverting more water from rivers and pumping additional water from underground aquifers. But in many sections of the country our current water use is unsustainable. Our diversions of surface water have completely dried up some rivers and reduced the flow in others to a trickle. . . .

The second option for satisfying new water demands is expanding our available supply. Dams function essentially as storage reservoirs which ensure that water is available at a time when Mother Nature does not. In the American West, most water comes from winter snowfall in the mountains. During the spring thaw, the snowmelt creates cascading rivers that provide more water than farmers or cities need for that season. During the summer, when the water needs of farmers and cities increase, dams function to smooth out the supply.

Beginning with the construction of Hoover Dam in the 1930s, the American West embarked on a dam-building frenzy. The remarkable construction of Hoover Dam symbolized how the United States could do anything, even harness the mighty Colorado River. To a nation in the throes of the Great Depression, it was a welcome boost, personifying an ambition that promised a bright economic future. And the power for that future would come from dams, lots of them, each producing hydroelectric energy. The water aided western farmers, and the power enabled American companies, such as Boeing, Lockheed, and Martin Marietta, to become aerospace giants. By the end of the dam-building era in the 1960s, most major western rivers had been dammed, some repeatedly. Indeed, in the United States as a whole, there are 75,000 dams six feet or higher and as many as 2.5 million smaller dams. Fewer than 60 American rivers are free-flowing.

In the mid-20th century, it seemed inconceivable that there might be a downside to building dams. But there was. Decades later, we came to realize how profoundly dams alter watersheds. Dam construction inundated some of the most beautiful canyons in the West, such as Hetch Hetchy and Glen Canyon, and transformed the rivers below the dams. Water flowing from a dam has a constant temperature as opposed to one that fluctuates with the seasons. Most dams increase water temperatures, but some decrease temperatures as they release cold water from the bottom of the reservoir. The flow itself depends on the decisions of engineers, not on a natural rhythm. Native fish and other aquatic species suffer from these changes when the nutrients that formerly sustained the downstream aquatic habitat become trapped in the quiet lakes upstream. . . .

Are there other options to expand our water supply? Desalination of ocean water offers the prospect of solving the lament of [19th century author] Samuel Taylor Coleridge's ancient mariner: "Water, water, everywhere" but not "a drop to drink." Removing salt from ocean water to make it potable offers a tantalizing possibility of an abundant new source of water. Some middle eastern countries and Caribbean Islands have obtained drinking water from desalination plants for a long time. In 2001, Tampa Bay Water began construction of the largest desalination plant in the Western Hemisphere. The $110 million plant came online in March 2003 and was expected to produce 25 million gallons of potable water per day. Alas, the plant only operated for two weeks before problems cropped up. . . .

Water Recycling and Conservation Are Options

The third option for satisfying new water demands, one that is technically viable today, is the reuse of municipal effluent. Historically, cities dumped raw sewage into our rivers. Today, most household wastewater, whether from toilets or showers, ends up at the municipal wastewater treatment facility. Until recently, this facility would filter the water under the standards mandated by the federal Clean Water Act and then discharge it into a nearby river. From the city's perspective, the point was to get rid of it as cheaply as possible without generating litigation or complaints about odors. Now, ironically, effluent has economic value. Many industrial users realize that effluent provides a perfectly adequate water supply, joining farmers who have used effluent for crops and cities that have used it for golf courses, municipal parks, cemeteries, and roadway medians. Indeed, wastewater treatment technology can take sewer water and clean it up to drinking water quality, though most Americans would rather not dwell on this prospect. In 1998, San Diego floated a trial balloon along these lines, but the program—dubbed, by some, the "Toilet to Tap" proposal—was dead on arrival. Squeamishness aside, astronauts have lived with total water-recycling programs since the beginning of the space program. In any event, using municipal effluent for purposes other than drinking water would expand our water supply. Yet the treatment process is quite expensive and delivery of effluent for nonpotable purposes requires a completely separate set of pipes and valves—a daunting financial prospect for cash-strapped American cities. Effluent reuse will help, but not solve, the problem of finding an adequate quantity of water to supply the increasing demands of a larger population.

As a fourth option, we could make our existing supply last longer by using water wisely and efficiently. The impetus for water conservation might come from two directions: government rules and regulations or market-based price signals. An example of government rules and regulations is Arizona's Groundwater Management Act, which imposes on all users—cities, farms, and mines—conservation standards that are phased in over 45 years. In each successive ten-year period, the standards tighten like a ratchet, requiring more effort from the users to comply. After 25 years of experience, the results are mixed. . . .

An alternative water conservation strategy would gain people's attention about their water use through their pocketbooks. If the price of water rose, people would carefully examine how they use water, for what purposes, and in what quantity. Alas, the price of water in the United States is ridiculously low. Many Americans pay more for their cell phones and cable television each month than they pay for water. Whether a consumer receives water from a municipal water department or from a private company regulated by the state public utility commission, the bill that she receives is only for the "cost of service"—those costs associated with delivering the water. There is no commodity charge for the water; it is literally free because water departments and utilities do not pay for the water themselves, and they pass that benefit along to consumers. This will change when cities are forced to acquire new supplies by entering the market to purchase water rights from willing sellers at market rates. But for the moment, existing water bills do not reflect these new costs. . . .

Key Option Is Creation of Markets to Move Water Away from Inefficient Agricultural Uses

Desalination, effluent reuse, water conservation, and water pricing will help secure additional supplies and reduce demand in the future. But the pressure to find more water continues. Where will the water come from? We cannot make more water because the hydrologic cycle is a closed one. That leaves a fifth option for satisfying new demands: we can reallocate water from current uses to new ones. We are about to enter an era of water reallocation. How will this reallocation take place? The government could mandate transfers from one user to another, except that would generate bitter political controversy and litigation over whether the government has the authority to act so cavalierly and whether the Constitution prevents the confiscation of water rights.

It would be far better to encourage voluntary transfers between willing sellers and buyers. Let them decide what the water is worth to each of them. Water markets would facilitate the movement of water from low-value activities to higher-value ones, thus resulting in a more efficient deployment of the resource. In the United States, we waste an immense amount of water growing cotton and alfalfa to feed cattle. In California, farmers grow cotton on 750,000 acres, heavily subsidized by the federal government. Irrigation systems are often primitive earthen canals that lose 40% to 50% of the water diverted into them through seepage into the ground. Once the water arrives at a farm, many farmers use highly inefficient flood irrigation or sprinkler irrigation with nozzles directing the water into the air where much of it evaporates. By one measurement, almost one million acre-feet of the three million acre-feet diverted by the Imperial Irrigation District in southern California ends up as wastewater flowing into the Salton Sea. In the United States, farmers irrigate millions of acres of marginal land, not because they produce high yields or generate substantial profits—in fact they do not—but because the farmer has the right to irrigate. Indeed, failure to do so may result in losing the water right through the doctrines of abandonment or forfeiture. Although some farmers have adopted water-saving technologies, agricultural subsidies and water subsidies combine to distort the economics of agricultural production. As a result, many farmers persist in growing low-value crops and fail to reduce the waste of artificially devalued water resources.

Current System Needs an Overhaul

This byzantine system needs a major overhaul. Part of this reform should come from government rules and regulations that impose conservation requirements, eliminate subsidies, encourage investment in modernization, and require "full-cost pricing"—the beneficiaries of U.S. Bureau of Reclamation projects should pay the actual cost of the water they receive. But these changes, each desirable in the abstract, would be extraordinarily difficult to execute in the concrete. Several involve very expensive system improvements, such as lining canals with concrete or laser-leveling fields that can cost hundreds of thousands of dollars for a single farm. Where is this money to come from, given that many farmers operate on razor-thin margins? Because the price of food relative to inflation has remained stable since the 1940s, it is a wonder any farmers can make a go of it. As a sardonic expression about making money in farming puts it, "If you want to make a small fortune in farming, start with a large one." It is not feasible, reasonable, or equitable to require farmers to undertake massive expenditures in order to make their irrigation systems more efficient. Even if it were reasonable, it will not happen for one very practical reason: farmers yield immense political

To Save Water, Sell It

It's way past time for wasteful farmers to get out of the way of other California industries. Farming consumes 80% of the water used in the state, but as an industry it produces less than 3% of the state's income. Some farmers might even be willing to be paid to get out of the way, but a bewildering cloud of rules often prevents them from selling or trading their water rights.

Thomas G. Donlan, "To Save Water, Sell It,"
Barron's, *August 4, 2008.*

power. State legislators would act at their peril were they to require their farmer constituents to shoulder the burden of these huge expenses. As the doctrine of public choice instructs, politicians like to remain in office. . . .

Recognizing this political reality, we must accept the fact that state legislators will not impose costly changes on the farming community. The best way to reform agricultural water use in the United States is to give farmers a financial incentive to use less: let them sell water to cities.

Let Farmers Sell Water to Cities

Market-based transfers can take many forms, from sales to leases, from forbearance agreements to dry-year options, and from land fallowing to conservation measures that save water. Each offers the prospect of a win-win result as the seller secures a price that she finds attractive and the buyer secures a water supply worth the negotiated price. The case for water marketing rests on the assumption that ownership of an item invests the owner with an incentive to take care of it. While this is surely not a universal proposition—as human beings span a range from the most obsessive-compulsive among us to those who seem oblivious to disarray, and from those who find it difficult to part with a nickel to those who cannot seem to hold on to one—ownership still changes behavior. Consider rental cars and ask yourself whether you would treat a new car that you purchased the same way you treat a rental car. When, for example, was the last time you washed a rental car? The same point might be made about hotel rooms, public parks, and parking lots. I have never seen a cigarette smoker dump his ashtray out in his driveway, but some smokers do not hesitate to do so in parking lots.

An ability to transfer ownership creates an incentive to use property more productively. This is the core idea of markets. Owners of property assess the value of it to them and part with it if they will realize a profit. Buyers seek to change the use of property and capture the value added by the new use. In this process, both sellers and buyers make profits, and society benefits from increased efficiency.

Water Markets Provide Many Benefits

Water markets have other benefits. They permit the reallocation of water in response to changes in population and economic development. To take one example, the computer industry in California's Silicon Valley has transformed the American economy and required that we find water for those who work in the information technology field and for the industries that make the chips and routers that fuel the web. In California, 1,000 acre-feet of water generates 9,000 jobs in the semiconductor industry but only 3 jobs producing cotton. Each acre-foot used by the semiconductor industry produces nearly $1 million in gross state revenue but only $60 growing cotton and alfalfa. At the same time, NAFTA [North American Free Trade Agreement] and other international trade agreements have opened American markets to agricultural powerhouses in Latin America and Asia, putting pressure on our farmers who have watched their margins erode. The time is ripe for some farmers to transition out of growing crops whose economic yield does not warrant the time, effort, and money that it takes to grow them. Water markets provide them this option.

Water markets may even encourage water conservation. If a farmer who reduces water loss by lining his ditch with concrete can profit from the sale of water he has conserved, it stimulates the investment in conservation practices and frees up the water saved for other users. The environmental community has also come to recognize the potential benefits of water markets. The transfer of water from farms to cities lessens the pressure to build new dams, to divert even more surface water, and to pump more groundwater. And it has allowed some environmental groups to purchase water rights from farmers that they then dedicate to in-stream flow rights, thus ensuring minimum flow levels in sensitive rivers and streams.

Let's be clear about one thing: we are talking about transfers from rural farming areas to cities. Most of the water that will sustain the expected 15 million additional Californians is going to come from agriculture. It has to. In California, as in most western states, farmers use between 70% and 80% of the state's fresh water. One cannot seriously address the question of new demands for water without focusing on agriculture. Another driving factor is money. In many western states, a high percentage of agricultural water is used to grow cotton and alfalfa, crops that return a relatively low value. The economic value of this water to cities dwarfs the value of the same water to the farmers. It makes economic sense to let the water support the higher value activity.

If water markets are to flourish, there must be a system of quantified water rights that are transferable. Water markets can only develop if a farmer has a known and fixed right that she can sell or lease. Without a property right that is quantified and transferable, there will be no voluntary reallocation of water use.

Government Must Oversee Water Transfers

The state should not give unrestricted permission to transfer water. Water is a public good and a public resource. The transfer of water from agriculture to cities will benefit both farmers and urban interests, but it may harm third parties. Communities have developed around agricultural centers to serve the farms and to provide a pool of labor to maintain the agricultural economy. If a farmer sells water to a city, his decision has implications for his farm workers; his John Deere dealer; his pesticide, fertilizer, and seed suppliers; and his lawyer, accountant, and banker. Also affected are local restaurants, supermarkets, and retailers who provide necessities and small luxuries to low-wage agricultural workers. Even local government will suffer financially from lost or lowered property values, sales, and income taxes, and from the increased need to provide social services to displaced workers. Equity demands that the beneficiaries of the water transfer compensate all those hurt by it.

Government must oversee the transfer process by setting standards regarding who is entitled to compensation, for what, and for how long. The trick will be to ensure fair compensation for those harmed by the transfer without creating a cumbersome hearing and appeal process that would drive up transaction costs and hijack the transfer process.

Government must also ensure that environmental factors receive careful consideration. Market systems have difficulty internalizing environmental costs. Economists expect that a rational owner of private property will protect the environment on his own property. But a water transfer may affect the habitat on someone else's property, such as the land of a downstream neighbor or a state wildlife refuge. For water transfers to become a legitimate tool for water reallocation, they must internalize both third-party and environmental costs. Even then, government may occasionally prohibit water transfers in order to protect valued and unique communities. For example, northern New Mexico's *acequias* are centuries-old subsistence-farming communities of Hispanic Roman Catholics that conceive of water as a community resource. The State of New Mexico has a compelling interest in protecting this rich culture's traditional water use. . . .

Addressing the problem of water scarcity will require action on a number of fronts. We must encourage the reuse of municipal effluent, explore the technological boundaries of water desalination, impose appropriate conservation requirements, and raise water rates. We must also recognize the reality of private rights in water and embrace water marketing as a critical tool to reallocate water use. In this process, the government must play a critical role in overseeing water transfers to protect the interests of third parties and the environment.

| "*Permanently removed from agricultural lands and rural areas, water diversions to cities can harm rural economics.*"

The Impacts of Water Transfer on Rural Communities Must Be Considered

Tyler McMahon and Matthew Reuer

In the following viewpoint, Tyler McMahon and Matthew Reuer assert that agricultural-to-urban water transfers can pose problems for rural communities. McMahon and Reuer say that these types of transfers are becoming increasingly common because farmers can get more money selling their water than they can get selling agricultural crops. McMahon and Reuer say that when water transfers completely remove land from agricultural use, the economic vitality of rural communities is harmed. Mc-Mahon and Reuer believe that creative water-sharing options exist to outright water transfers, which can help satisfy cities' thirst for water and maintain the vitality of rural farming communities. Colorado College issued the first State of the Rockies Report Card *in 2004. The Report Cards provide annual statements about the most pressing issues of the Rocky Mountain States*

Tyler McMahon and Matthew Reuer, "Water Sustainability in the Rockies," *The 2007 Colorado College State of the Rockies Report Card*, 2007. Reproduced by permission. www.coloradocollege.edu.

(Arizona, Colorado, Idaho, Montana, Nevada, New Mexico, Utah, and Wyoming). McMahon is a class of 2007 Colorado College (CC) student, and Reuer is the technical director for the CC Environmental Sciences Program and coeditor of the State of the Rockies Report Card.

As you read, consider the following questions:

1. According to McMahon and Reuer, what percentage of the Rockies' population was classified as urban in 2000?

2. According to McMahon and Reuer, what two factors have strongly affected agricultural economics?

3. In what year did the Colorado Supreme Court establish the legal precedent for water transfers in that state? What city received the water from this transfer?

4. What are three of the alternative transfer methods that McMahon and Reuer say can benefit both town and country?

Water—or more specifically the lack of it—has greatly shaped the American West. From the early settlers lured by the promise that "rain follows the plow" to recently arrived suburbanites expecting lush lawns and fountains in desert communities, access to clean, reliable water has dominated the region's economy, culture, and settlements. In the *2007 Colorado College State of the Rockies Report Card* we examine water allocation in the Rockies, with emphasis on current water use patterns and agriculture to urban transfers.

The Rockies: Little Precipitation and Fast-Growing Cities

The eight-state Rockies Region receives on average 30 inches of annual precipitation. However, as any resident or visitor to the Rockies knows, water availability varies widely by place, season, and year. Winter alpine snowpack melts into streams, rivers, and reservoirs, with some of this water diverted as far away as California or the eastern flank of the Rockies. In other places, scarcely any precipitation falls, and agriculture or human settlement would be impossible without a massive water transfer and pumping infrastructure. Las Vegas, for example, with its continuously running fountains and green golf courses, receives less than five inches of precipitation per year. Rocky Ford, Colorado, a town discussed later for its transfer of water rights to the city of Aurora receives less than 12 inches a year. . . . To compensate for low and sporadic precipitation, the region has historically transferred water from areas of abundance (e.g., areas of alpine snowpack, major rivers, or aquifers) to areas of scarcity (semi-arid plains and deserts). These water transfers are increasingly important as urban areas rapidly develop in arid and semi-arid climates. . . .

Although present water use in the Rockies is dominated by irrigation, . . . future regional population growth will likely exceed that in other regions and will be concentrated in urban areas. The Rockies Region includes many of the fastest-growing states in the U.S., such as Nevada, Arizona, Colorado, Utah and Idaho. Despite its rural agricultural heritage, 83 percent of the Rockies population was classified as urban in 2000, and this percentage continues to increase. However, agricultural water use is much greater than current urban water consumption. For the Rockies Region, just 7 percent of agricultural water use is equivalent to twice the municipal water use in 2000, and this percentage varied from 1 percent in Montana to 30 percent in Nevada. Further development of urban areas will increase demands for the region's limited water, likely removing more water from agriculture while also requiring greater urban conservation efforts for a sustainable future.

Water Transfers Can Harm Rural Communities

New urban water demands, combined with historically low agricultural commodity prices, have allowed urban financial resources to out-bid agriculture, resulting in transfers of water from agriculture to cities. These water transfers may involve the purchase or lease of agricultural water rights by municipalities. Permanently removed from agricultural lands and rural areas, water diversions to cities can harm rural economics by diminishing tax revenue, reducing retail trade associated with agriculture, and spurring emigration of rural residents. But creative new tools and techniques are being developed to help urban and rural areas successfully coexist by sharing water.

While these tools are being developed, both sides must examine their water consumption and the associated impacts on water supply and quality. Sprinkler irrigation of agricultural fields, for example, can result in water losses of only 20 percent, depending on the relative humidity, air temperature, wind speed, and irrigation system used. Agricultural practices use can also degrade water quality, via nitrate runoff from fertilizer use, pesticide runoff associated with weed or disease control, and salinization of discharge water. Urban areas also often use water in ways that flout conservation concerns. Thirsty lawns and evaporative losses consume more than half of domestic household water use in arid climates. For example, outdoor water use in Scottsdale, Arizona, accounts for 72 percent of residential water consumption. Urbanization can also degrade water quality, through storm-water discharges, industrial releases of aquatic toxins, and sewage discharges. . . .

Poor Agricultural Economics Spurring Water Transfers

Water use data collected by the USGS [United States Geological Survey] indicate the importance of agricultural water use in the Rockies. One option to address urban water supply problems is agricultural water transfers. Water transfers from agricultural to urban uses have been increasing in Western states due to urban growth, the declining agricultural economy, and groundwater overdraft concerns. Other pressures on traditional water supplies include recent drought, fully appropriated rivers (where all water is reserved for existing water rights and other legal requirements such as interstate compact delivery requirements), and the decline of federal funding for large water projects. The lack of new water projects results in no additional storage capacity, providing abundant surface water during early spring but limited supplies in late summer.

Agricultural economics has been strongly affected by two factors: the decline of agriculture's profitability relative to other sectors and the concentration of agricultural operations into larger and more efficient units. In 1940, farm employment accounted for 26 percent of total employment in the Rockies, whereas in 2003 farm employment equaled only 2.6 percent of total employment. The average farm size in the Rockies has also increased due to mechanization and economies of scale. In 1920, the average farm size was 528 acres, compared to 2,034 acres in 2000 (the historical maximum was 3,043 acres in 1975). More efficient, larger farms and improvements in agricultural technology and inputs have led to higher crop yields and lower commodity prices, which have, in turn, promoted larger farms. Drought, natural disasters, and crop and livestock diseases have forced many smaller farms and ranches out of business. For example, melon growers in Rocky Ford, Colorado, have suffered from low prices, storm damage, a salmonella scare, recurring drought, and warmer temperatures that harmed critical crops. The significant economic pressures placed on agriculture over the last several decades have increased the importance of agriculture to urban water transfers.

Another motivation for agricultural water transfers is the ownership of senior water rights by Western farmers and ranchers. Since the early 1900s, most of the rivers in this region have been fully appropriated. To obtain a new water source, a city must purchase water rights from another entity (unless the city already owns undeveloped rights). The market value of the water right is largely determined by seniority. Seniority is based on the year the water right was established (known as the "priority date" or "appropriation date"): an 1865 water right is senior to an 1870 water right. Each year, the water user with the most senior right may use their full allocation, assuming the water source can provide it. Then the user with the next senior right can use their allocation, and so on. In times of water scarcity, junior right holders might not receive part or all of their allocation. Because the Homestead Act of 1862 attracted ranchers and farmers to Western lands in close proximity to rivers, these early settlers generally obtained the most valuable, senior rights. . . .

As noted above, irrigation currently dominates water use in the Rockies. However, farmers have suffered both from natural events such as droughts and from economic factors such as low profit margins. Given the scarcity of Western water resources, the transfer of water from agriculture to cities could be an important means of addressing water availability problems. The "agricultural reservoir" is the largest existing source of water in the Rockies, but such transfers have long-term implications and it is unknown how they will affect rural economies and communities.

The Evolution of Western Water Transfers

Water transfers have a long history in the Rockies and have evolved since the 19th century. Early transfers were known as "water farming," by which cities would purchase a farm, leave the land fallow or lease water back to an irrigator while waiting to convert the associated water rights. In 1891 the legal precedent for transfers in Colorado was established by the Colorado Supreme Court, approving an irrigation water transfer to Colorado Springs. In the 1970s and 1980s, the cities of Aurora and Thornton, Colorado, bought most of the irrigation water rights in rural South Park, Colorado, approximately 90 miles to the southwest. In Arizona, water farming became more and more common with groundwater depletion in the 1970s and 1980s.

With the declining economic importance of agriculture, water rights have become a sort of pension or bail-out plan for many farmers in the Rockies. However, the drying up of agricultural land has significant implications for rural economies. One example is the property tax base of Morgan County, Colorado. In 2006, 400 junior wells were shut down to protect senior surface water rights, with estimated property value losses of $30 million as once-irrigated lands were reclassified as dry land.

The secondary costs of water transfers have spurred public outcry in rural areas and increased awareness of equity issues. Following the 1985 transfer of Rocky Ford Ditch water from rural Rocky Ford to urban Aurora, Colorado, the city of Aurora addressed third-party impacts of the water transfer by re-seeding the affected land with native plants and compensating rural Otero County for lost tax revenue as irrigated lands were reclassified as lower value dry lands. While many cities have pursued various types of equitable solutions to water transfers, the general public frequently blames the region's growing cities and limited conservation efforts. However, lower commodity prices are what promote water transfers for struggling farmers. That in turn degrades the rural economy and further pushes small operators off the land.

Rural Communities Respond Differently to Water Transfers

Although the agricultural sector has declined in economic importance in the Rockies, agricultural areas have responded quite differently to the economic impacts of water transfers. Howe and Goemans studied the impact of water transfers in the South Platte Basin and Arkansas river basin of Colorado.

Drying out Rural Farming Communities

Ray Colbert wanted out after five decades of growing apples, but his son didn't want the farm in northern Washington. No one else did either.

So, Colbert sold the last big piece of his operation, an 80-acre parcel, to a buyer far downstate who wanted what came with the land: water from the Okanogan River.

State regulators signed off on the buyer's request to transfer the rights to the water and let it flow hundreds of miles downriver, figuring the deal was good for fish and wouldn't hurt anyone else's water supply.

Local officials, however, fear such deals will dry out their rural farming community.

"If this were to snowball and keep up, Okanogan County would literally dry up. It would dry up its economy, its agricultural production and everything else," said State Sen. Bob Morton, a Republican whose rural district sprawls across remote northern Washington.

Several factors related to water transfers and the regional economy contributed to a much larger impact in the Arkansas Basin than in the Platte basin. Specifically, the economic impacts depended on (1) the size of the transfer; (2) the vitality of the region's pre-transfer economy; and (3) the ultimate destination and use of the transfer (e.g., inside or outside the basin, new water use or not). In the Arkansas Valley, 88 percent of the water transfers were large (114,320 acre feet were transferred from 1980–1995 and left the basin). In contrast, in the South Platte Basin, transfers were generally smaller and stayed within the basin. The Arkansas River Basin also had a less robust pre-transfer economy than the Platte River basin. The resulting impacts on income and taxes in the basins were estimated at $187 per acre foot and $83 per acre foot, respectively.

The concentration of agriculture also affects the economic impact of water transfers. For example, in the six counties in Colorado's Lower Arkansas Valley (Bent, Crowley, Las Animas, Otero, Pueblo, and Kiowa), the proportion of farm income (1 percent) was double the Colorado average (0.5 percent) for 2004; excluding Pueblo County, the region's farm income jumps to 6 percent of total personal income. This demonstrates the importance of agriculture in the Lower Arkansas Valley. In past decades, this area has experienced large water transfers from the basin, including the Rocky Ford purchases and a 100,000 acre-foot purchase from the Colorado Canal (1985). . . . Although such transfers provide short-term economic benefits to struggling farms, the long-term and regional impact of lower tax revenues, weaker retail sales, and population losses threaten the economic vitality of the Arkansas Valley.

Alternative Water Transfer Strategies Can Benefit Town and Country

Water transfers need not harm rural areas to provide water to a municipality, and new water strategies have been developed to benefit both town and county. Some of the methods that have been developed include interruptible supply agreements, rotational fallowing (or "crop management") arrangements, water banking, alternative cropping or irrigation practices, and purchase/lease-back arrangements. Cities have also initiated conservation programs to extend their water supplies and limit drought impacts.

Interruptible supply agreements (ISAs) allow cities (or other water users) to contract with water rights holders for use of the right in times of drought. . . .

Rotational crop management agreements are established by a group of farmers who agree to periodically fallow portions of their lands, transferring a consistent water supply to the buyer. These agreements provide supplemental annual base water sources to urban areas, reduce demands on aquifers, and decrease agricultural land dry-up rates. . . .

Water banking is another useful transfer tool. Water banks serve as an intermediary between water users and rights holders, allowing unused water rights to be leased for present or future use. Water banks allow users to store excess water for their own future use and protect against excess water loss. . . .

Another water transfer tool is alternative crops or water conservation measures. By reducing their consumptive use (e.g., by converting alfalfa to drought-tolerant grasses or adopting new irrigation methods), farmers can increase revenue by selling the water they save. . . .

An additional water transfer strategy is called "purchase and lease back," where a municipality purchases land or its associated water rights and then leases them back to the land's user (such as a farmer or third party). The municipality gains access to some or all of the water in the future. . . .

Many of these strategies offer positive alternatives to permanent loss of agricultural land, which often has unexpected consequences for growing urban areas. For example, near Phoenix, Arizona, the open space buffer created by surrounding farms reduces the urban heat island effect and mitigates the city's higher surface temperatures. Rotational crop management arrangements could help address micro-climate issues by keeping most farms in production every year and alternating the amount of fallow land. For farm operators, benefits of fallowing include rotational crop management payments that may then be invested in potential improvements to field irrigation systems and improvements (e.g., laser-leveling) that will increase future water conservation.

Urban Water Needs Are Urgent; However, We Must Maintain Our Rural Community

Despite the increasing trend toward agriculture to urban water transfers, supplying clean water to the Rockies' growing population remains an urgent problem. As previously discussed, the number of irrigated acres in the Rockies decreased (6 percent) between 1997 and 2002. While most water use in the Rockies Region is devoted to irrigation (87.2 percent in 2000) and adequate water exists for urban transfers, agricultural land is declining faster than anticipated. In Colorado, the Statewide Water Supply Initiative (SWSI) estimated that while the state's population may grow by 65 percent between 2000 and 2030 (1.7 percent per year), 185,000 to 428,000 irrigated acres could be lost by 2030 due to water transfer projects, urbanization of irrigated lands, and other agriculture water losses (adjusted for some potential increase in irrigated acres if new water supplies are developed). The 2002 Census of Agriculture estimate for irrigated land out of production (470,000 acres in 2002) does provide some context, but this estimate is based on a drought year, so some portion of this fallow land will likely return to production. The decline in irrigated land raises new concerns about the economic vitality of rural areas and the cultural heritage lost. Are we trading rural agricultural lands under cultivation for urban water uses that have higher market value? Can small farms thrive through equitable water transfers and the development of more efficient irrigation techniques? Conservation and creative water sharing methods can potentially benefit the Rockies' people, land, and environment, but the demands of a growing population will likely create new tensions.

> *"Ninety-seven percent of all water distribution in poor countries is managed by the public sector, which is largely responsible for more than a billion people being without water."*

Water Privatization Is a Good Idea

Fredrik Segerfeldt

In the following viewpoint, Fredrik Segerfeldt argues that water privatization can save lives in developing countries. According to Segerfeldt, the most important thing that can be done to decrease death and disease in water-poor countries is to get people connected to "water mains," so they don't have to buy unsafe and expensive water from small-time vendors. Segerfeldt believes private companies can do a much better job than government agencies in getting people connected to water mains. Water privatization is already saving lives in several countries, says Segerfeldt. Segerfeldt works at the Swedish free-market think tank Timbro and is the author of Water For Sale—How Business and Markets Can Resolve the World's Water Crisis.

Fredrik Segerfeldt, "Private Water Saves Lives," *Financial Times*, August 25, 2005, p. 11.

As you read, consider the following questions:

1. According to Segerfeldt, what kinds of groups have come together to form anti-privatization coalitions?

2. According to Segerfeldt, people without access to water mains usually purchase lower quality water from small-time vendors. How much more, on average, do they pay?

3. In which countries does Segerfeldt claim water privatization has already saved lives?

Worldwide, 1.1 billion people, mainly in poor countries, do not have access to clean, safe water. The shortage of water helps to perpetuate poverty, disease and early death. However, there is no shortage of water, at least not globally. We use a mere 8 percent of the water available for human consumption. Instead, bad policies are the main problem. Even Cherrapunji, India, the wettest place on earth, suffers from recurrent water shortages.

Private Businesses Are Better than Government

Ninety-seven percent of all water distribution in poor countries is managed by the public sector, which is largely responsible for more than a billion people being without water. Some governments of impoverished nations have turned to business for help, usually with good results. In poor countries with private investments in the water sector, more people have access to water than in those without such investments. Moreover, there are many examples of local businesses improving water distribution. Superior competence, better incentives and better access to capital for investment have allowed private distributors to enhance both the quality of the water and the scope of its distribution. Millions of people who lacked water mains within reach are now getting clean and safe water delivered within a convenient distance.

"You're such a thirsty bunch," cartoon by Ralph Hagen. www.CartoonStock.com.

The privatisation of water distribution has stirred up strong feelings and met with resistance. There have been violent protests and demonstrations against water privatisation all over the world. Western anti-business non-governmental organisations and public employee unions, sometimes together with local protesters, have formed anti-privatisation coalitions. However, the movement's criticisms are off base.

Arguments Against Privatization Are Flawed

The main argument of the anti-privatisation movement is that privatisation increases prices, making water unaffordable for millions of poor people. In some cases, it is true that prices have gone up after privatisation; in others not. But the price of water for those already connected to a mains network should not be the immediate concern. Instead, we should focus on those who lack access to mains water, usually the poorest in poor countries. It is primarily those people who die, suffer from disease and are trapped in poverty.

They usually purchase their lower-quality water from small-time vendors, paying on average 12 times more than for water from regular mains, and often more than that. When the price of water for those already connected goes up, the distributor gets both the resources to enlarge the network and the incentives to reach as many new customers as possible. When prices are too low to cover the costs of laying new pipes, each new customer entails a loss rather than a profit, which makes the distributor unwilling to extend the network. Therefore, even a doubling of the price of mains water could actually give poor people access to cheaper water than before.

There is another, less serious, argument put forward by the anti-privatisation movement. Since water is considered a human right and since we die if we do not drink, its distribution must be handled democratically; that is, remain in the hands of the government and not be handed over to private, profit-seeking interests. Here we must allow for a degree of pragmatism. Access to food is also a human right. People also die if they do not eat. And in countries where food is produced and distributed "democratically", there tends to be neither food nor democracy. No one can seriously argue that all food should be produced and distributed by governments.

The resistance to giving enterprise and the market a larger scope in water distribution in poor countries has had the effect desired by the protesters. The pace of privatisation has slowed. It is therefore vital that we have a serious discussion based on facts and analysis, rather than on anecdotes and dogmas.

Privatization Has Already Saved Lives—Don't Stop It, Make It Better

True, many privatisations have been troublesome. Proper supervision has been missing. Regulatory bodies charged with enforcing contracts have been non-existent, incompetent or too weak. Contracts have been badly designed and bidding processes sloppy. But these mistakes do not make strong arguments against privatisations as such, but against bad privatisations. Let us, therefore, have a discussion on how to make them work better, instead of rejecting the idea altogether. Greater scope for businesses and the market has already saved many lives in Chile and Argentina, in Cambodia and the Philippines, in Guinea and Gabon. There are millions more to be saved.

| "The evidence clearly shows that water privatization has been a disastrous policy for poor people around the word."

Water Privatization Is a Bad Idea

Wenonah Hauter

In the following viewpoint, Wenonah Hauter argues that water privatization is a bad idea. According to Hauter, in the places where private corporations have taken control of water distribution, such as Dar es Salaam, Ecuador, and Atlanta, it has been disastrous. Private water corporations have a bad track record says Hauter, which includes firing essential workers, jeopardizing safety, delivering poor-quality water, and causing sewage spills. Hauter believes water is too important to allow multinational corporations to make a profit on it. It should be delivered by the government at low cost, says Hauter; it is, after all, a human right. Hauter is the director of Food and Water Watch, a non-profit consumer organization working to ensure clean water and safe food.

As you read, consider the following questions:

1. According to Hauter, in the United States today, public utilities provide what percentage of household drinking water and what percentage to sewer services?

2. According to Hauter, what is the name of the private water company that must pay millions of dollars to the East African country Tanzania under the ruling of an international tribunal?

3. According to Hauter, how old are many of the drinking water and sewer systems in the United States?

If adequate water for drinking and sanitation is essential for life, shouldn't we consider water a human right? Not everyone thinks so. In February [2008], the United Nations Human Rights Council missed a critical opportunity to recognize a human right to water. As a result of lobbying by the United States and Canada, the council derailed a European-backed declaration, accepting instead a weaker resolution that actually protects a corporation's right to sell water.

Water as a Profit Center

As illustrated by the February United Nations vote, our government and its corporate allies believe that water is a new profit center. They are promoting markets and privatization as the solution to providing water to the world's poor—1.4 billion people without access to drinking water and 2.5 billion without sanitation services. International finance institutions, funded by the United States and other developed nations, provide loans to developing nations on the condition that they privatize services and charge steep user fees. Indeed, the very institutions that are charged with alleviating poverty, like the World Bank, are implementing policies that force people who make $1 or $2 a day to choose among food, housing, or water.

Contrast this with the United States where, at the turn of the 20th century, reformers concerned about the high levels of water-borne disease successfully campaigned for public funding of municipal water and sewage systems. Today, public utilities provide 86 percent of household drinking water and 98 percent of sewer services. But the same economic interests promoting privatization in the developing world are clamoring for it in the United States.

Over the past 15 years, private water corporations, mostly European, have begun targeting American cities for privatization. Equity research firms predict that privatization of water services and private investment in pipes and infrastructure could provide large and stable profits. Proponents of privatization cite economic efficiency as one of its biggest selling points. But studies by independent researchers and even dissenting voices within the World Bank refute this claim.

A Record of Empty Promises

Communities all over the world have suffered from the empty promises of water-privatization profiteers. Whether in Dar es Salaam, Tanzania, or Guayaquil, Ecuador, or Atlanta, the results have been devastating. They include cost-cutting measures that jeopardize public safety, job cuts to essential staff, maintenance and water quality problems, lack of infrastructure investment, sewage spills, corruption, environmental degradation, outrageous rate hikes, and political meddling.

Almost across the board, private corporations deliver poorer service at a higher cost than do most public utilities. Surveys of U.S. utilities show that privately owned water utilities charge customers significantly higher water rates than their publicly owned counterparts charge—anywhere from 13 percent to almost 50 percent more, according to an analysis by Food & Water Watch, the advocacy group I direct. The reality is that any "efficiency" is realized by firing staff—often up to half of existing staff—undermining the ability of the utility to maintain pipes and other infrastructure.

Case studies from recent practices around the globe tell the story. In 2005, the government of Tanzania canceled its 10-year contract with the British-based firm Biwater after two years of poor management and unmet obligations left people without water and the government short about $3.25 million. The East African country enjoyed some measure of justice in early 2008 when an international tribunal ruled that Biwater must pay almost $8 million in damages and fees to the state water utility in Dar es Salaam. Not coincidentally, the company had taken control of the city's water supply in a controversial, noncompetitive privatization process favored by the British government and the World Bank. One critic was quoted as saying: "The evidence clearly shows that water privatization has been a disastrous policy for poor people around the world, but the World Bank insisted on imposing water privatization in Tanzania in return for much needed debt relief."

Halfway around the world, the same disastrous model also was foisted upon the people of Ecuador. There, the wheels were set in motion by the Inter-American Development Bank (IDB), whose lending policies are as damaging as those of the World Bank because they require privatization of water utilities without considering restructuring and rehabilitating public utilities. In this case, the IDB loaned $40 million to the government of Ecuador to prepare a subsidiary of the U.S.-based contracting giant Bechtel to operate the water and sewer system in the country's largest city, Guayaquil.

Shortly after the subsidiary, which became known as Interagua, took over in Guayaquil in 2001, it dismissed all the workers from the previously public-owned utility. The company partially bowed to public pressure by rehiring 20 percent of them the following year. But mass firings were only one installment of the nightmare. The media reported in 2002 that Interagua was treating only 5 percent of the sewage and releasing the rest directly into the Guayas River. The Guayaquil health department began issuing reports of skin ailments, including rashes; respiratory problems such as asthma; and diarrhea and other gastric illnesses. Authorities found that Interagua's poor service also contributed to a major outbreak of Hepatitis A in 2005.

Unfortunately, a similar story can be told by communities across Latin America. The World Bank and IDB provided loans to Bolivia for water and sewer systems in its capital, La Paz, and neighboring El Alto, only on the condition that private companies supply these services. In 1997, Aguas del Illimani, led by Paris-based Suez, the world's second largest water and wastewater corporation, obtained a 30-year contract to operate the cities' water and sewer systems, but by 2005 long-festering anger over massive rate hikes and poor service contributed to public protests, a general strike, and social unrest.

The contract written by the company had "red lined" poorer neighborhoods, leaving 200,000 people without water services. In addition, some 80,000 families who should have been served were denied water. A connection fee of $450—a poor family's food budget for two years—was charged to hook up to water and sanitation services. The Bolivian government audited the company's performance and found it had not complied with the contract, had not made the required investments in infrastructure, and had a dismal environmental performance.

Rough Waters in America

Sadly, Suez and the other water corporations have had a similar record in the United States. United Water, a Suez subsidiary, began a 20-year, $428 million contract in 1999 to operate and manage Atlanta's water and sewer system. At the time, United Water bragged that "Atlanta for us will be a reference worldwide, a kind of showcase."

Instead, a fiasco ensued. The company overstated the amount of money it could save the city and underestimated the work needed to maintain and operate the system. In At-

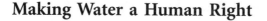

Making Water a Human Right

Ensuring that access to sufficient safe water is a human right constitutes an important step towards making it a reality for everyone. It means that:

- fresh water is a legal entitlement, rather than a commodity or service provided on a charitable basis;

- achieving basic and improved levels of access should be accelerated;

- the "least served" are better targeted and therefore inequalities decreased;

- communities and vulnerable groups will be empowered to take part in decision-making processes;

- the means and mechanisms available in the United Nations human rights system will be used to monitor the progress of States Parties in realizing the right to water and to hold governments accountable.

World Health Organization,
"The Right To Water," 2003.

lanta, the company cut costs by firing almost 400 employees—half of the utilities staff. United Water tried to add $80 million to the contract and then, after the city refused, inflated billable costs, even billing the city for work it hadn't performed. It raised sewer rates an average of 12 percent every year it had the contract.

There were other problems, as well. In 2003, the city's deputy water commissioner told *The Atlanta Journal-Constitution*, "My biggest concern is a lot of people have lost confidence in the water itself. Over the past year, we've had so many boil water advisories and discolored water around the system." Finally fed up with United Water, Atlanta terminated the contract later that year.

In other cases, concerned citizens are fighting back. The town of Emmaus, in Pennsylvania's Lehigh Valley, is one such example. Facing costly repairs and improvements in their public water system, borough leaders in 2005 entertained bids from private corporations, promising that proceeds from the sale of the town's water supply would be invested in tax cuts for residents. Then came the bad news: The prospective corporate buyer would likely raise rates by three or four times.

A grass-roots effort soon mobilized, urging the town council to "stop the corporate water grab" and "save our water for future generations." Paul Marin, one of the organizers, remembers asking: "Why turn this or any other public resource that the community already owns and has paid for over to a private entity? You're paying twice. It's like selling your house and then paying the buyer's mortgage over the next 30 years."

Eventually, town leaders relented, and Emmaus kept its water. Rates did go up enough to restore the town's water fund and buy needed upgrades, but customers are still paying among the lowest water prices in the state.

Unfortunately, the happy ending for Emmaus does not ensure public control of water in other American communities. Private corporations continue to approach local leaders with promises to repair water infrastructure and increase efficiency.

Public Funding, Not Privatization, Because Water Is a Human Right

Indeed, in the United States, our drinking water and sewer systems, many of which are more than 100 years old, do need upgrades. The Environmental Protection Agency estimates that we are falling short on water-infrastructure funding by a whopping $22 billion yearly. Fortunately, a real solution does exist. Instead of allowing irresponsible private-investment schemes, we need to plan ahead for future generations by creating a dedicated source of public funding so that communities across America can keep their water clean, safe, and affordable. Water is a vital resource, critical for all of us. It deserves no less than the trust funds that currently help finance our highways, harbors, and wildlife habitats. It is time for a federal trust fund for clean and safe water.

And in the developing world, it's time for a new model. The answer to providing safe, affordable drinking water and sewer services to developing nations is not giant corporations. It's time that the world's richest nations, including our own, use their influence to change the policies of the international finance institutions they fund. The World Bank and the IDB should stop predicating their loans on privatization. These powerful institutions must stop forcing poor countries to structure their economies in a way to benefit multinational corporations, and instead prioritize public health and increased access to clean and affordable water for all people. Because water is, after all, a human right.

> "The Great Lakes Compact represents a historic step forward in Great Lakes water policy."

The Great Lakes Compact Is a Success

Noah D. Hall

In the following viewpoint, Noah D. Hall describes the key elements of the Great Lakes Compact and deems it a success. The Great Lakes Compact is a state law in each of the eight states that are within the Great Lakes Basin—Illinois, Indiana, Michigan, Minnesota, New York, Ohio, Pennsylvania, and Wisconsin. It is also a federal law, having been enacted by U.S. Congress and signed into law by President George. W. Bush on October 3, 2008. A similar but nonbinding agreement was also signed between the Great Lakes states and the Canadian Provinces of Ontario and Québec. The Compact prevents water from being diverted out of the Great Lakes basin, with some limited exceptions. It also provides minimum standards for conservation and environmental protection of water in the Great Lakes. According to Hall, the compact is a major step forward in water law, as it is the first time both surface (i.e., lakes and rivers) and ground

Noah D. Hall, "Testimony: Interstate Water Management and the Great Lakes-St. Lawrence River Basin Water Resources Compact," United States Senate Committee on the Judiciary, Hearing on S.J. Res 45, July 30, 2008. Reproduced by permission of the author. www.greatlakeslaw.org.

(i.e., underground aquifers) water are recognized as a single resource. It also provides a model of state and federal cooperation for other states to use in managing shared water resources. Hall believes the compact represents a historic agreement that will protect the Great Lakes and ensure that states are using its water wisely. Hall is a professor at the Wayne State University Law School in Detroit, Michigan, and the director of the Great Lakes Environmental Law Center.

As you read, consider the following questions:

1. According to Hall, why is it critical for the eventual success of any Great Lakes water policy that ground and surface water are addressed?

2. The Great Lakes Compact creates two separate approaches for managing new or increased water withdrawals. What is the differentiation in the two approaches based upon, according to Hall?

3. According to Hall, what size water bottle container is defined as a diversion under the Great Lakes Compact?

This section summarizes and analyzes the key provisions of the Great Lakes-St. Lawrence River Basin Water Resources Compact (hereinafter "Great Lakes Compact").... The Great Lakes Compact is a binding agreement between the eight American states that have jurisdiction over the Great Lakes. Under the Great Lakes Compact, the world's largest freshwater resource would be protected and managed pursuant to minimum standards administered primarily under the authority of individual states. The Great Lakes Compact puts riparian[1] water use rules and environmental protection standards into a proactive public law regime. The standards represent numerous advances in the development of water use law, including

1. Riparian refers to the land adjacent to water.

uniform treatment for ground and surface water withdrawals, water conservation, return flow, and prevention of environmental impacts. . . .

Compact Addresses Ground and Surface Water

At the core of the Great Lakes Compact is the common standards (referred to as the "decision-making standard") for new or increased water withdrawals of Great Lakes basin water. The applicability of these standards is not limited to water taken directly from one of the Great Lakes. Rather, the Great Lakes Compact broadly defines the waters of the Great Lakes to include all tributary surface and ground waters. Just this initial recognition of connected ground water and surface water as a single resource to be managed uniformly is a long overdue advancement in water law. Addressing both ground and surface water is also critical to the eventual success of any Great Lakes water policy, since ground water comprises over fifteen percent of the total water supply in the Great Lakes basin.

While the decision-making standard applies broadly to all waters, it only applies to new or increased withdrawals of water. This follows the express scope of Annex 2001.[2] Existing uses are not grandfathered or protected by the compact; individual jurisdictions are simply free to regulate (or not regulate) existing uses as they see fit. While existing withdrawals are not regulated under the Great Lakes Compact, states are required to implement "a voluntary or mandatory" water conservation program with state-specific goals and objectives for all water users, including existing users.

2. Annex 2001 refers to an agreement signed by Great Lakes governors and Canadian premiers in 2001. It is called an Annex because it reaffirmed a previous agreement, the Great Lakes Charter, and added new commitments.

Criteria for Making Decisions About Great Lakes Water

The decision-making standard contains the following criteria for new or increased water withdrawals:

1. All Water Withdrawn shall be returned, either naturally or after use, to the Source Watershed less an allowance for Consumptive Use;

2. The Withdrawal . . . will be implemented so as to ensure that [it] will result in no significant individual or cumulative adverse impacts to the quantity or quality of the Waters and Water Dependent Natural Resources [of the Great Lakes Basin] and the applicable Source Watershed;

3. The Withdrawal . . . will be implemented so as to incorporate Environmentally Sound and Economically Feasible Water Conservation Measures;

4. The Withdrawal . . . will be implemented so as to ensure that it is in compliance with all applicable municipal, State and federal laws as well as regional interstate and international agreements, including the Boundary Waters Treaty of 1909;

5. The proposed use is reasonable, based upon a consideration of the following factors:

   • Whether the proposed Withdrawal . . . is planned in a fashion that provides for efficient use of the water, and will avoid or minimize the waste of Water;

   • If the Proposal is for an increased Withdrawal . . . , whether efficient use is made of existing supplies;

   • The balance between economic development, social development and environmental protection of the proposed Withdrawal and use and other existing or planned withdrawals and water uses sharing the water source;

- The supply potential of the water source, considering quantity, quality, and reliability and safe yield of hydrologically interconnected water sources;

- The probable degree and duration of any adverse impacts caused or expected to be caused by the proposed Withdrawal and use under foreseeable conditions, to other lawful consumptive or non-consumptive uses of water or to the quantity or quality of the Waters and Water Dependent Natural Resources of the Basin, and the proposed plans and arrangements for avoiding or mitigation of such impacts; and,

- If a Proposal includes restoration of hydrologic conditions and functions of the Source Watershed, the Party may consider that.

Criteria Founded on "Reasonable Use," Conservation, and Environmental Law

These criteria have discernable roots in common law riparian rules and the doctrine of reasonable use. Criteria (5)(a)—(e) follow closely the factors for determining reasonable use as described in section 850A of the Restatement (Second) of Torts.[3] Further, water conservation—criterion (3)—has long been recognized as a factor in determining the reasonableness of water use under riparian law. Even criterion (2), which prevents a water withdrawal from having "significant" adverse environmental impacts, has a base in common law riparian rules.

Despite the Great Lakes Compact's generally limited focus on managing and regulating only new or increased water uses, criterion (5)(b) requires consideration of "efficient use . . . of existing water supplies." If applied strictly, a community could not obtain approval for an increase in its water withdrawal to

3. The Restatement of Torts (Second Version) is an influential document, which summarizes general principles of tort law.

meet the needs of a growing population without first implementing conservation measures for its existing uses. Similarly, a manufacturer or irrigator that wishes to expand and increase its water use must first take measures to reasonably reduce its current water use through conservation practices. Through this criterion, the compact could force efficiency improvements and water conservation on many existing users as they expand, encouraging a "hard look" at existing water use practices and methods. Finally, criterion (5)(f) allows consideration of proposals to restore "hydrologic conditions and functions" in the source watershed. Thus, watershed improvements are not strictly required, but can be considered in the overall determination regarding the reasonableness of the proposed use. Water users can propose a restoration or improvement as a way of making their water use more compatible with the resources and limitations in the watershed.

The Great Lakes Compact makes clear that the common decision-making standard is only a minimum standard. States may impose more restrictive standards for water withdrawals under their authority. Some jurisdictions (such as Michigan and Minnesota) already have permitting standards in place, and this ensures that the compact in no way requires a weakening of state regulatory programs.

The Great Lakes Compact's decision-making standard is a major evolution in eastern water law. While it represents historic progress in the advancement of water resources law, it is also grounded in common law riparian rules and various environmental statutes. However, environmental standards are only as good as the management and enforcement systems by which they are applied. Fortunately for the Great Lakes, the Great Lakes Compact provides a meaningful system of interstate water management and enforcement to ensure that the standards are applied across the Great Lakes basin.

The Great Lakes Compact creates two separate approaches to managing new or increased water withdrawals in the Great Lakes basin. The differentiation is based almost entirely on whether the water is used inside or outside of the Great Lakes basin surface watershed boundary. Water use inside of the Great Lakes basin is managed solely by the individual state, with limited advisory input from other states for very large consumptive uses. Water use outside of the basin (a diversion) is subject to a spectrum of collective rules and approval processes, including a general prohibition on most diversions.

Management of Water Use Inside the Basin

The Great Lakes Compact requires the states to "create a program for the management and regulation of New or Increased Withdrawals . . . by adopting and implementing Measures consistent with the Decision-Making Standard" within five years. States must set the threshold levels for regulation of water withdrawals to "ensure that uses overall are reasonable, that Withdrawals overall will not result in significant impacts . . . and that all other objectives of the Compact are achieved." If states fail to establish thresholds that comply with these requirements, a default threshold of regulating all new or increased withdrawals of 100,000 gpd or greater (averaged over any ninety-day period) is imposed. The states must make reports to the Compact Council, which is comprised of the governor of each party state, regarding their implementation. The Compact Council must then review the state programs and make findings regarding their adequacy and compliance with the Great Lakes Compact.

The states must further develop and promote water conservation programs in cooperation with the Compact Council within two years of the effective date of the Great Lakes Compact. While not specifically regulatory, the state programs are intended to advance the Great Lakes Compact's goals, including protecting and restoring Great Lakes hydrologic and eco-

system integrity. Through their respective conservation programs, states must promote water conservation measures such
as "[d]emand-side and supply-side [m]easures or incentives."

Finally, the states are required to develop and maintain a
water resources inventory with information regarding both
available water resources and water withdrawals within the
state. As part of this requirement, all water users (both existing and new) making water withdrawals greater than 100,000
gpd (averaged over any ninety-day period) must register with
their state and report the details of their water use. The information gathered by the individual states will create a regional
common base of data for interstate information exchange.
This information is critical to both state and interstate management of the Great Lakes, especially with regards to cumulative impacts of water withdrawals.

Management of Diversions

The simplest form of interstate management under the Great
Lakes Compact is the general prohibition on new or increased
diversions of Great Lakes water. Diversions are defined to include both the transfer of Great Lakes basin water into another watershed (interbasin diversion) as well as diversions
from one Great Lake watershed into another Great Lake watershed (intrabasin diversion). However, this broad definition
belies one of the three major exceptions to the prohibition on
diversions: intrabasin transfers.

While not subject to the prohibition on diversions, intra-
basin transfers are subject to the "exception standard" and
varying state approvals and additional requirements based on
the amount of the withdrawal and consumptive use. Intrabasin transfers below 100,000 gpd (averaged over any 90-day
period) are left solely to the discretion of the individual state.
Intrabasin transfers above the 100,000 gpd threshold but with
a consumptive use below 5 million gpd are subject to state
management and regulation based on the exception standard,

as well as the prior notice process for comments by other states. Intrabasin transfers with a consumptive use above 5 million gpd are subject not only to state regulation pursuant to the exception standard and a non-binding regional review process, but also to the unanimous approval of the Compact Council (comprised of each of the governors).

Straddling Communities and Counties

The other two exceptions to the prohibition on diversions involve communities and counties that straddle the surface water basin divide. Sprawling metro areas that have expanded beyond the Great Lakes watershed are a contentious issue in the region. For example, while the city of Milwaukee sits on the shores of Lake Michigan, its suburbs now go beyond the Lake Michigan surface watershed, which is only a few miles from the lakeshore in some areas of Wisconsin. It is important to recognize, however, that the communities just outside the surface watershed are often still within the ground watershed, and may in fact be using ground water connected to the Great Lakes. Thus, both socially and scientifically, these communities could be fairly considered part of the Great Lakes basin.

The Great Lakes Compact addresses this issue by bringing straddling communities and counties that use Great Lakes surface water for public water supply purposes into the management regime. A straddling community, defined as an incorporated city or town that uses Great Lakes water for public supply purposes both inside and outside of the surface water basin, is treated similarly to an in-basin withdrawal, subject to state regulation pursuant to the exception standard. To prevent exploitation of this exception by growing incorporated cities and towns through mergers and annexations, the Great Lakes Compact limits the defined straddling community to the boundaries existing as of the effective date of the compact.

A proposal for a diversion in a straddling county, which encompasses a far greater area than a "community," is subject to additional standards and regional approval. First, the water can be used solely for the public water supply purposes of a community that is without "adequate supplies of potable water." Second, the proposal is subject to an additional "cautionary" standard, requiring a showing that the proposal "will not endanger the integrity of the Basin Ecosystem." Finally, the proposal is subject to both non-binding regional review and the unanimous approval of the Compact Council.

The Question of Bottled Water

The question of whether bottled water shipped out of the basin constitutes a diversion has been an emotional political topic in recent years. Some environmental activists view bottled water as no different from a tanker or pipeline that sends water to distant markets for private profit. The bottled water industry views itself as an in-basin consumptive use, creating a product (bottled water) from a natural resource. Both arguments are perched on slippery slopes. Environmental activists view bottled water as opening the door to massive private sale of the Great Lakes. Industry sees no difference between bottles filled with pure water and bottles filled with water and a little sugar, corn syrup or artificial flavor (also known as soft drinks, or "pop" in the Midwest). The question of whether bottled water constitutes a diversion is so loaded with political controversy that the governors decided not to conclusively address it in the Great Lakes Compact. While the Great Lakes Compact defines water in containers greater than 5.7 gallons (20 liters) as a diversion, it leaves the decision of how to treat water in containers of 5.7 gallons or less to the individual states.

Duties and Powers of the Compact Council

In addition to providing a mechanism for unanimous approval of the diversion exceptions, the Compact Council has numerous other powers and duties. Comprised of the gover-

Building a Wall Around the Great Lakes

The Milwaukee suburb of New Berlin gets half its water from the Great Lakes and half from underground wells that are tainted with radium, a radioactive element.

The city of 38,500 has a simple solution to its water problem: draw more water from Lake Michigan, 10 miles away. That probably won't happen.

New Berlin may look like a typical Midwestern suburb, but it's really a border town—on the edge of the Great Lakes watershed—and the west side of town is on the wrong side of the water slope.

A new multistate agreement working its way through state legislatures builds a legal wall around the largest source of fresh water in the world. The deal would ensure that no Great Lakes water is ever shipped outside the region—not in pipes to Arizona, not in ships to Asia, not even to Madison, Wis., or Columbus, Ohio.

Dennis Cauchon,
"Great Lakes Compact at the Center of Great Debate,"
USA Today, December 10, 2006.

nors of each party state (or their designated alternates), it can promulgate and enforce rules to implement its duties under the Great Lakes Compact. The Compact Council also has broad authority to plan, conduct research, prepare reports on water use, and forecast water levels. Perhaps most importantly, it can conduct special investigations and institute court actions, including enforcement.

Enforcement is not the sole domain of the Compact Council, however. The Great Lakes Compact contains broad and comprehensive enforcement provisions at both the state and interstate levels. Any aggrieved person can commence a civil enforcement action in the relevant state court against a water user that has failed to obtain a required permit or is violating the prohibition on diversions. Remedies include equitable relief and the prevailing party may recover reasonable attorney and expert witness fees. Any person, including another state or province, can challenge a state action under the Great Lakes Compact (such as issuance of a permit) pursuant to state administrative law, with an express right of judicial review in state court.

The broad enforcement provisions are complemented by similarly progressive public participation provisions. As with the minimum substantive decision-making standard, the compact provides minimum procedural public process requirements for the party states and Compact Council. These include: public notification of applications with a reasonable time for comments; public accessibility to all documents (including comments); standards for determining whether to hold a public meeting or hearing on an application; and allowing open public inspection of all records relating to decisions. The Great Lakes Compact also requires additional formal consultation with federally recognized Tribes in the relevant state. In recognition of the Tribes' status as sovereigns, such consultation is handled primarily through either the Compact Council or Regional Body.

The Great Lakes Compact becomes effective once ratified through concurring legislation in each party state (which has now occurred) and consented to by Congress [occurred in 2008]. The Great Lakes Compact has no termination date; it remains in force unless terminated by a majority of the party states (five of the eight). As is typical for interstate water compacts, it is very difficult to amend once enacted. Amendments would require unanimous approval by all state legislative bodies and the consent of Congress....

A Historic Step Forward

The Great Lakes Compact represents a historic step forward in Great Lakes water policy. The decision-making standard alone is a major evolution in water law. The unified management of surface and ground water brings some scientific reality to the law. And the provisions for enforcement, public process, and cooperation with Canadian provinces ensure more accountable and participatory decision making. However, the mechanism through which these standards and provisions are applied may be the most important advancement. The Great Lakes Compact introduces a new cooperative horizontal federalism approach for crafting multi-state water resource and environmental policy that could be a model for future environmental policy efforts.

> *"Despite many positive aspects to the proposal, it utterly fails to promote the ecological health of the Basin and its water and water dependent resources."*

The Great Lakes Compact Is Flawed

Mark S. Squillace

In the following viewpoint, Mark Squillace contends that the Great Lakes Compact is flawed. Squillace says the major flaw of the compact is that it focuses too much attention on preventing new consumptive uses (where water is permanently removed from the Basin) and completely ignores existing uses of Great Lakes water. According to Squillace, existing uses of Great Lakes water, such as the diversion of the Chicago River into the Mississippi River and dredging in the St. Clair and Detroit Rivers, already have a far more significant impact on the levels of the Great Lakes than any new consumptive use might have. Squillace says other problems with the compact are that it is overly complicated, it intrudes on state authority, and it doesn't pay enough attention to upper watersheds. Squillace doesn't think the compact meets the goals set forth in previous Great Lakes agree-

Mark S. Squillace, "Rethinking the Great Lakes Compact: How the Compact Fails to Protect the Great Lakes," *Michigan State University Law Review*, 1347:5, 2006, pp. 1347–74. Reproduced by permission. http://papers.ssrn.com.

ments to protect, conserve, restore, and improve the waters of the Great Lakes. Squillace is the director of the Natural Resources Law Center at the University of Colorado School of Law.

As you read, consider the following questions:

1. According to Squillace, the compact only addresses new withdrawals that occur after the deadline for establishing a regulatory program. When is the deadline?

2. According to Squillace, what was the name of the company that wanted to ship Lake Superior water out of the Great Lakes Basin in 1998? Where was the water supposed to go?

3. According to Squillace, Nestlé Waters North America pumps water from a well in western Michigan, which is hydrologically connected to what water resource?

Before describing the fundamental problem with the proposed [Great Lakes] compact, it is necessary to look back at the core motives that led to its development. While it may be appropriate to ascribe protectionism as at least one underlying reason for the proposed compact, the professed and most prominent reason for the effort was a sincere desire to protect the ecological values inherent in the water resources of the Great Lakes. Evidence of this comes from both the original 1985 Charter and the 2001 Annex [agreements preceding the compact]. . . . The key reasons for the Charter were "to conserve the levels and flows of the Great Lakes and their tributaries and connecting waters, [and] to protect and conserve the environmental balance of the Great Lakes." The Annex commits the parties to develop "an enhanced water management system . . . that most importantly, protects, conserves, restores, and improves the waters and water dependent natural resources of the Great Lakes basin."

Ignoring Existing Uses Is a Major Flaw of the Compact

The proposed compact can thus be fairly assessed in terms of whether it achieves these overarching goals. Sadly, it does not. Despite many positive aspects to the proposal, it utterly fails to promote the ecological health of the Basin and its water and water dependent resources. The key feature of the proposed compact is its requirement that states manage new or increased withdrawals, and assess them against a specific decision-making standard. For many reasons, this cumbersome requirement is unlikely to achieve any progress toward protecting lake levels and promoting the ecological health in the Basin. Most importantly, by focusing so much attention on new or increased withdrawals, the proposed compact ignores all of the far more significant existing uses and activities that currently affect the water resources of the Great Lakes Basin. In a report published in 2000, the IJC [International Joint Commission][1] described how existing uses currently impact the Great Lakes. That impact illustrates how insignificant the new or increased withdrawals are likely to be on the water resources of the Great Lakes for many years to come.

Several existing projects have impacts on lake levels that far exceed the impacts from all of the existing consumptive uses from all of the states and provinces through 1993. Most strikingly, the dredging of the St. Clair and Detroit Rivers alone has an impact on Lakes Michigan and Huron that is more than fifteen times the impact of all the existing consumptive uses for those bodies of water. All of the existing consumptive uses have a comparatively minor impact on lake levels when compared with the other diversions and projects. Of course, the proposed compact will not address any of the uses or projects, since it focuses almost exclusively on *new* consumptive uses. But a compact that addresses only new

1. The International Joint Commission (IJC) was created under the 1909 Boundary Waters Treaty to prevent and resolve disputes between the U.S. and Canada.

withdrawals—indeed, new withdrawals that occur after the deadline for establishing a regulatory program, which is five years from the compact's effective date—and that ignores existing withdrawals and other uses and activities that significantly impact lake levels cannot hope to achieve the ecological health goals that are set forth in the Charter and Annex.

Compact Is Complicated and Disrespectful of State Authority

Beyond the goal of protecting and conserving the waters of the Great Lakes Basin, the Annex mandates a solution that is "simple, durable, efficient, [and] retains and respects authority within the Basin. . . ." But the highly specific standards for evaluating new withdrawal applications cannot be simply applied, and the complex assessment that the compact requires states to make to ascertain compliance with the standards cannot be done efficiently. Most importantly though, the "command and control" directive to regulate new water withdrawals pursuant to detailed criteria does not respect state authority. Even assuming that consideration of the cumulative impact of consumptive uses might be necessary to protect and conserve the water resources of the Great Lakes Basin, the rigid system imposed under the compact on every state for new water uses is certainly not the only, and arguably not the best way to conserve water resources. For example, rather than regulating new uses strictly, some states might prefer to relax their standards on new uses and regulate existing uses modestly to achieve even better conservation overall than provided for under the compact. Moreover, because the compact imposes no firm cap on overall use of the water resources of the Basin, the potential for overuse under the compact model remains. Indeed, because the equitable position of the parties favors increasing their use as against each other, one would expect the compact to promote, rather than restrain, consumption of water resources, notwithstanding the detailed process for approving consumptive uses. If the parties are truly committed to respecting state authority, and if the most important thing is to protect the water resources of the Great Lakes, then States should be free to adopt any plan that achieves an appropriate level of water conservation.

The Compact's Handling of Diversions Is Problematic

In the spring of 1998, the Nova Group based in Sault Ste. Marie, Ontario proposed annual shipments by tanker of 160 million gallons of Lake Superior water to Asia. Although Ontario initially approved the proposal, the province quickly reversed course after a public outcry against it. More importantly, the proposal prompted renewed efforts by the Great Lakes states and provinces to revisit the Great Lakes Charter. The 2001 Annex, and the proposed compact that followed, are a direct result of those efforts.

Long before the Nova Group's proposal, however, the parties had wrestled with the problem of out-of-basin diversions. The Water Resources Development Act [WRDA] of 1986 had effectively blocked most new out-of-basin diversions, and despite the problems this legislation had created for some communities located within basin states but outside the Basin, a substantial constituency developed to fortify the ban on most diversions.

The proposed compact imposes a strict ban on new diversions that in some respects goes beyond the provisions of WRDA. Whereas WRDA allowed diversions so long as every Great Lakes governor approved them, the proposed compact bans all diversions except in narrow circumstances. As noted previously, limited exceptions are authorized for straddling communities and straddling counties, as well as for intra-basin transfers. In particular, out-of-basin diversions are allowed only for public water supplies, and any water withdrawn from the Basin must be returned to the source watershed less an allowance for consumptive use. Moreover, a single state can veto any diversion proposed by straddling counties as well as large intra-basin diversions. Parties must submit to a Regional Review for these large diversions as well that includes all of the Great Lakes states and provinces.

While it is surely important to prevent massive out-of-basin diversions that can directly impact water levels of the lakes, such as the Chicago River Diversion, it is far from clear that the states or provinces should have any control over diversions that fail to impact them in any measurable way. Why, for example, should Michigan or Ohio have any role to play in a proposal by Quebec or New York to divert water out of the St. Lawrence Seaway? Why too, should any state or province be allowed to object if another state or province prefers to judiciously use some of its fair share of Great Lakes water for an out-of-basin purpose? Under the proposed compact, states may not object to another state's overuse of Great Lakes water resources so long as those uses are in the Basin and the state follows the compact's procedures for approving their use. Yet over the long term, such uses could have a far greater impact on the Great Lakes and the balance of uses among the states and provinces, than any out-of-basin diversion. In other words, the compact focuses too much on the place of the use, rather than on the impact of the use on the overall water resources in the Basin.

By severely limiting use of Great Lakes water out of the Basin, the proposed compact also indirectly promotes extractions within smaller watersheds and groundwater basins, where the potential for ecological damage may be far more severe. For example, a community outside the Basin that fails to qualify as a straddling community or county faces an outright ban on Great Lakes water use. Yet the compact fails to reveal even the slightest recognition that withdrawals from a local watershed or groundwater basin could have a significant local ecological impact, whereas the use of Great Lakes water in the same amount might well be negligible. This problem could arise even with straddling communities and counties, since the proposed compact provides significant disincentives to such communities that might want to withdraw Great Lakes water, including requirements to conduct an alternatives analysis, undergo regional review, and return water to the source watershed after use. It is entirely appropriate that the proposed compact considers the ecological health of the Great Lakes, but it is wrong to essentially ignore the broader ecological impact on the affected region, as the proposed compact does. Indeed, because the local watersheds adjacent to the Great Lakes Basin will necessarily be much smaller, the potential for ecological harm to these adjacent watersheds from withdrawing a fixed amount of water is far higher.

Upper Watersheds Left Unprotected

Under the proposed compact, the states and provinces are required to ensure that "withdrawals overall will not result in impacts to the waters and water dependent natural resources, determined on the basis of significant impacts to the physical, chemical, and biological integrity of the source watersheds. . . ." In addition, withdrawals and consumptive uses must be implemented "so as to ensure that the proposal will result in no significant individual or cumulative adverse impacts to the quantity or quality of the waters and water dependent natural resources." While these provisions could, and perhaps should, be construed to restrict proposals to remove waters from upper watersheds, they are certainly not framed in those terms, and they are worded so generally that they will be easy to circumvent. As previously argued, the proposed compact is fairly criticized for being unduly intrusive on state authority without a commensurate benefit. Yet, the one place where intrusion on state authority may make sense is for such upper watershed withdrawals. Anecdotal evidence from recent

Agreement

Section 1. The states of Illinois, Indiana, Michigan, Minnesota, New York, Ohio and Wisconsin and the Commonwealth of Pennsylvania hereby solemnly covenant and agree with each other, upon enactment of concurrent legislation by the respective state legislatures and consent by the Congress of the United States as follows:

Great Lakes—St. Lawrence River Basin Water Resources Compact

Article 1

Short Title, Definitions, Purposes and Duration

Section 1.1. Short Title. This act shall be known and may be cited as the "Great Lakes—St. Lawrence River Basin Water Resources Compact."

Section 1.2. Definitions. For the purposes of this Compact, and of any supplemental or concurring legislation enacted pursuant thereto, except as may be otherwise required by the context:. . .

Basin or **Great Lakes—St. Lawrence River Basin** means the watershed of the Great Lakes and the St. Lawrence River upstream from Trois-Rivières, Québec within the jurisdiction of the Parties.

Basin Ecosystem or **Great Lakes—St. Lawrence River Basin Ecosystem** means the interacting components of air, land, Water and living organisms, including humankind, within the Basin.

The Great Lakes—St. Lawrence River Basin Water Resources Compact, December 13, 2005.

water supply controversies suggests that this is really where the ecological problems are most likely to occur.

For example, several years ago the Michigan Citizens for Water Conservation sued Nestlé Waters North America for pumping water for a water bottling plant in western Michigan. The well from which the water was extracted was hydrologically connected to Sanctuary Springs, which connects to the headwaters of the West Branch of the Little Muskegon River. The trial court found that the water resources below the pumping site were impaired at pumping rates above 160–170 gallons per minute. Nestlé wanted to pump at an average rate of 250 gallons per minute, or 360,000 gallons per day. The difference—about 90 gallons per minute, or 129,600 gallons per day—is, by most measures, a small amount of water. If this water had been taken directly from one of the Great Lakes, or from an aquifer directly connected to one of the Lakes, the impact would have been negligible. By taking the water from the upper watershed of a small tributary, however, the withdrawal may well have a significant ecological impact. The proposed compact would do much more to protect the ecological health of the Great Lakes if it had focused on banning upper watershed withdrawals rather than out-of-basin diversions. Yet it lacks any specific limit on such uses.

Compact Should Be Redesigned

If the focus of the compact were truly on managing the Basin's water resources to protect its ecological health, then the states and provinces should design a management framework that addresses the large withdrawals, uses, and activities that either individually or cumulatively have a meaningfully impact on lake or tributary stream levels. These should include activities such as the dredging of the St. Clair River, the operation of the Welland Canal, the Chicago River diversion, and the Long Lac and Lake Okogi diversions. While it may be politically and practically impossible to significantly alter these activities, the proposed compact could give ownership of these activities to the host state or province in a way that would promote their better management. As Justice [Oliver Wendell] Holmes [Supreme Court Justice 1902–1932] noted many years ago, "[a river] offers a necessity of life that must be rationed among those who have power over it." In keeping with this advice, the parties should allocate the water resources of the Great Lakes Basin based upon current levels of use. Unlike the proposed compact, such a framework would, in the words of the Charter Annex, offer a solution that is "simple, durable, efficient," and that "retains and respects authority within the Basin, and . . . protects, conserves, restores, and improves the waters and water dependent natural resources of the Great Lakes Basin."

Periodical Bibliography

Robert W. Adler
"Revisiting the Colorado River Compact: Time for a Change?" *Journal of Land, Resource and Environmental Law*, vol. 28, no. 1, 2008.

Charles Ashby
"McCain: Renegotiate 1922 Western Water Compact," *The Pueblo Chieftain*, August 15, 2008. www.chieftain.com.

Susan Berfield
"There Will Be Water," *Business Week*, June 12, 2008. www.businessweek.com.

Greg Bluestein
"Forgotten Ga. County Now in Spotlight Over Water Rights," *USA Today*, April 28, 2008. www.usatoday.com.

Tim Jones
"Fate of Great Lakes' Water Looking Fluid," *Los Angeles Times*, October 28, 2007. http://articles.latimes.com.

Farmers Guardian
"Finding Balance Between Profitable Farming and Protecting Environment," February 15, 2008.

Bill Holman and Richard Whisnant
"Will N.C. Have Enough Water?" *Greensboro News Record*, April 2, 2009. www.news-record.com.

Willie Howard
"Lake Worth to Vote on Water-Sharing Agreement with Palm Beach County," *Palm Beach Post*, April 6, 2009. www.palmbeachpost.com.

Richard Howitt and Kristina Hansen
"The Evolving Western Water Markets," *Choices*, First Quarter, 2005. www.choicesmagazine.org.

Brian Lavendel
"The Fourth Coast: National Parks Within the Fragile Great Lakes Ecosystem Face Serious Environmental Threats," *National Parks*, Fall 2006.

Carol Navorro and Mairin MacDonald
"Who Owns the Water?" *EJ Magazine*, Spring 2006. www.ejmagazine.com.

 OPPOSING
VIEWPOINTS®
SERIES

CHAPTER 4

Is Drinking Water Safe?

Chapter Preface

What is in your medicine cabinet? Toothpaste, mouthwash, and shaving cream are common items. It probably contains some out-of-date antibiotics, an analgesic, or leftover pain medication from a recent injury. Suntan lotion, cosmetics, hair dye, shampoos, ointments and creams, decongestants, and cough medicine are probably there, too. Many of these items may seem innocuous to the common person, but scientists are concerned that the items in many Americans' medicine cabinets are ending up in a very unexpected place—the water we drink.

Americans take a staggering amount of over-the-counter and prescription drugs. Analgesics like aspirin, acetaminophen, or ibuprofen are staples in American households. A typical household purchases these items at least four times each year. According to Medco Health Solutions, Inc., 51 percent of American adults and children were taking one or more prescribed pharmaceutical drugs in 2007. These drugs include painkillers, tranquilizers, antidepressants, antibiotics, birth control pills, and cholesterol drugs. Most of these drugs are not completely metabolized by the human body. This means that when a woman taking birth control pills goes to the bathroom, for example, her urine contains a significant amount of the female hormones estrogen and progestin. These unmetabolized pharmaceuticals end up in municipal wastewater or a homeowner's septic system. Similarly, residues of personal care products such as cosmetics, shampoos, sunscreens, and soaps are washed down the drain when people bathe and end up in municipal wastewater or septic tanks.

Pharmaceuticals and personal care products, referred to as PPCPs, make their way from municipal wastewater and septic tanks into soil and aquatic environments, and eventually end up in the water that comes out of the kitchen faucet. Conventional wastewater treatment does not remove most PPCPs, so they end up being discharged into lakes or leached into groundwater. PPCPs typically do not dissolve or evaporate easily. Therefore, they tend to persist in the environment and eventually make their way into the water sources municipalities use to obtain drinking water. Many of these PPCPs slip through the filters at drinking water treatment plants, which are designed to clean the water and make it fit for drinking. As a result, the tap water piped to many American homes contains PPCPs.

In March 2008, an investigative report by the Associated Press (AP) brought the issue of PPCPs in drinking water into the national spotlight. The AP found dozens of PPCPs in the drinking water of an estimated 41 million Americans. In the course of a five-month investigation, the AP discovered that tiny amounts of PPCPs had been detected in the drinking water supplies of twenty-four major metropolitan areas. Fifty-six pharmaceuticals or their byproducts, including pain killers, antibiotics, and medicines for high cholesterol, asthma, epilepsy, and mental illness, were found in the Philadelphia drinking water system. Anti-epileptic and anti-anxiety medications were detected in a portion of the treated drinking water sent to 18.5 million people in Southern California. The AP investigation was reported in newspapers across the country and received national attention.

Although the AP report was troubling, the prevalence of pharmaceuticals and the remnants of personal care products in water is nothing new. In the early 1990s, scientists in Europe detected clofibric acid, a cholesterol lowering drug, in the groundwater there. According to the U.S. Environmental Protection Agency (EPA), "PPCPs have probably been present in water and the environment for as long as humans have been using them. The drugs that we take are not entirely absorbed by our bodies, and are excreted and passed into wastewater and surface water. With advances in technology that improved the ability to detect and quantify these chemicals, we can now begin to identify what effects, if any, these chemicals have on human and environmental health."

Scientists don't yet know if the tiny amount of PPCPs found in drinking water poses a risk to human health. The concentrations of PPCPs found in drinking water are miniscule, measured in quantities of parts per billion or trillion— equivalent to one drop of water diluted into 250 chemical drums or one drop of water diluted into twenty two-meter-deep Olympic-sized swimming pools. According to the EPA, to date, scientists have found no evidence of adverse human health effects from this level of PPCPs. The same small levels of PPCPs in the environment, particularly hormone-related PPCPs, however, have been blamed for various negative effects on aquatic life, such as feminization of male fish. Scientists are working diligently to more thoroughly understand the impact of low levels of PPCPs on the environment and to understand and quantify the long-term risks to human health.

The safety of the water we drink is of paramount importance to us all. Some people trust that the water coming out of the tap is safe for drinking, while other people avoid tap water for various reasons and instead drink bottled water. As the authors in the following chapter demonstrate, there are many differing opinions on the safety of drinking water.

> *"There has been broad scientific and medical consensus for decades that one part per million of fluoride is best for health, and exactly zero rigorously conducted scientific trials that have indicated any sign of danger."*

Fluoridation of Public Drinking Water Is Beneficial

Brian Dunning

In the following viewpoint, Brian Dunning says fluoridation of public drinking water systems is an accepted and safe practice used to prevent dental decay. Dunning says there are numerous scientific studies to support maintaining fluoride levels of one part per million in drinking water. Zero studies support claims that fluoridation of drinking water is unsafe. Dunning blames a small, but vocal, group of conspiracy theorists for alarming the public about fluoridation of drinking water. Dunning says each one of their claims is false. He hopes that communities follow the lead of Arcata, California, and reject the anti-fluoridation lobby's attempts to ban fluoridation of municipal drinking water. Dun-

ning is a self-proclaimed skeptic. He is a featured blogger on SkepticBlog *and is the host of an upcoming TV series called* The Skeptologists.

As you read, consider the following questions:

1. According to Dunning, what was the name of the Colorado dentist who first noticed fluoride's effect on teeth?

2. According to Dunning, what was the name of the proposal to ban fluoridation in Arcata, California, which was crafted by the anti-fluoridation lobby?

3. As described by Dunning, in Europe, fluoride is not added to water, but is added to what?

Today we're going to wrap our big juicy lips around the kitchen faucet, turn on the valve, and fill our bodies with a poisonous chemical placed in our water by the government: fluoride.

Fluoridation Means Adjusting the Fluoride Content to the Most Healthful Level

Most people understand that fluoridation of water means that fluoride is added by the local municipal water supplier, and that's generally correct. What most people don't know is that in some cases, fluoridation means removing excess fluoride that occurs naturally in the water supply. Fluoride is a natural component of groundwater, and it occurs naturally everywhere in the world, in varying amounts. The process of fluoridation is to adjust the fluoride content of the water to the most healthful level.

So how did fluoridation become a normal part of municipal water supply? It all goes back to an early 20th century dentist named Dr. Frederick McKay, who practiced dentistry in Colorado, and noticed that a lot of his patients seemed to have brown teeth. In Texas, brown teeth were so prevalent that they were simply called "Texas Teeth". Dr. McKay spent 30 years investigating the cause. Why? Because it also turned out that people with Texas Teeth also had extremely low levels of dental decay. If you had brown teeth, you were only 1/3 as likely to have cavities.

Finally, in 1931, it was determined that naturally occurring fluoride in the local drinking water was responsible for both the discoloration and the lack of decay. Texas and Colorado had extremely high levels of natural fluoride, causing the discoloration, a condition now known as dental fluorosis, which is harmless if a tad unattractive. Years of research and testing in different cities and states, conducted by the National Health Service, determined that one part per million was the ideal proportion, giving the same protection from decay, and avoiding the dental fluorosis. Ever since then, it has been the standard practice to regulate fluoride levels in municipal water supplies to one part per million. There has been broad scientific and medical consensus for decades that one part per million of fluoride is best for health, and exactly zero rigorously conducted scientific trials that have indicated any sign of danger. For all practical purposes, it is an over-and-done-with issue.

A Campaign of Misinformation

And yet, like so many advances in science or medicine, fluoridation is criticized by a small yet vocal fringe group. There is absolutely an anti-fluoridation lobby in this country. Their process is to flood the mass media with as many claims as they can invent: Claims like fluoridation causes cancer or other illnesses; that insufficient research has been done or that there is "scientific controversy" surrounding fluoridation; that fluoride is a dangerous chemical poison; that fluoridation has been banned in Europe; that it eliminates your freedom of choice; or any of a dozen other baseless and untrue statements intended to alarm and frighten the public. Alarming the public is not hard to do. There are many communities in the United States where voters have been compelled to ban fluoridation by this widespread misinformation campaign.

Let's turn our eye onto one such community, Arcata, an idyllic coastal hamlet in northern California, that recently won this battle after a divisive and painful fight in the newspapers and in city hall. A principal champion of the science behind fluoridation is Kevin Hoover, editor of the *Arcata Eye* newspaper. In answering the flood of anti-fluoridation scare tactics, Hoover said:

> *There are no known victims. If there was a problem with municipal fluoridation, wouldn't we have at least a few people who showed some signs of harm after 44 years? All the anti-fluoride people could say was that the victims are "undiagnosed," but not why. They produced no victims, just lots of dubious statistics and horror stories with no provenance.*

Measure W to ban fluoridation was carefully crafted by the anti-fluoridation lobby to simply require FDA [Food and Drug Administration] approval of anything added to Arcata's water supply, which sounds reasonable and sounds like a good idea, and a layperson otherwise uninformed would be likely to vote for it. The catch is that the Food & Drug Administration has nothing whatsoever to do with municipal water supplies, and so of course FDA approval would never happen, by law. Measure W was essentially a devious, deceitful trick intended to further the anti-fluoridation lobby's agenda at the expense of the dental health of Arcata's children. Generally, it's this same tactic that has been responsible for most anti-fluoridation measures that have passed in the United States.

What They Don't Tell You

How else does the anti-fluoridation lobby go about spreading their misinformation? Generally they distribute an eight page pamphlet written by Dr. John Yiamouyiannis, the grandfather

CDC Says Fluoridation Is Safe and Effective

CDC [U.S. Centers for Disease Control & Prevention] recommends community water fluoridation as a safe, effective, and inexpensive way to prevent tooth decay (dental caries) among populations living in areas with adequate community water supply systems. Similar to many vitamins and minerals we consume for our health, fluoride should be taken in the proper amount. Past comprehensive reviews of the safety and effectiveness of fluoride in water have concluded that water fluoridation is safe and effective. Fluoride is present naturally in most water at a very low level, and more than 180 million people on public water systems in the United States enjoy the benefits of having their water adjusted to the optimal level (0.7–1.2 mg/L, or 0.7–1.2 parts per million [ppm]) for preventing tooth decay.

CDC Statement on the 2006 National Research Council (NRC) Report on Fluoride in Drinking Water, September 24, 2008. www.cdc.gov.

of anti-fluoridation activism. Dr. Yiamouyiannis was a naturopath who rejected modern medicine, and was the principal originator of the claim that fluoridation causes cancer. He raised his family with an emphasis on a fluoride-free diet to avoid cancer. And, as I'm sure you've guessed, Dr. Yiamouyiannis died of cancer in 2000, which he had refused to treat in accordance with his naturopathic philosophy. His type of cancer has a 95% 5-year survival rate, when properly treated.

Most other experts cited by activists are people like Dr. Hugo Theorell, who did indeed oppose fluoridation in the early days. What they don't tell you is that Dr. Theorell changed his mind and became a supporter after the research was published. They'll often cite Swedish Nobel Prize winner Arvid Carlsson, known for his work with dopamine. He's the only known Nobel Prize winner to oppose fluoridation, but the activists multiply him and frequently say that "dozens" or "many" Nobel Prize winners oppose it. When you can only find one guy who opposes something, and his work is in a completely different field anyway, that's a pretty sad commentary on your position. It's also a case of the exception proving the rule. There are always a few contrarian scientists in every field with opinions opposite from the consensus.

It's also stated that fluoridation adds dangerous levels of lead, arsenic, and mercury to the water. Again, this is simply untrue, and making such a claim is really a form of terrorism. In Arcata, no detectable levels of any of those are found in the fluoridated water. Not just below safe levels, mind you; zero.

You'll also hear the claim that fluoridation has been banned in Europe. This is also completely untrue. In Europe it's more common to fluoridate salt instead of water, thus bringing the same benefits via a different delivery method. As long as you don't look at that fact, the anti-fluoridation people can truthfully say that "Europe rejects fluoridation of water."

Thanks to the efforts of Hoover and all of Arcata's doctors, dentists, educators, social workers and newspapers, Measure W to ban fluoridation was soundly defeated in the election. And it's a good thing, too: according to sources in Arcata, if Measure W had passed, the same people were going to try and ban childhood vaccinations next.

Imaginary Conspiracy Theories

Why do they do it? We can really only speculate. Presumably most of these people are good citizens who love their families and want the best for everyone. I speculate that a lot of them are simply ignorant of the facts, and possibly mistrust of the government or anticorporatism compels them to tend to ignore information from official sources and embrace alternative claims, whatever their source. Hoover gave his own answer to this question in an editorial for the *Arcata Eye*:

> *Billion-dollar industries thrive around entirely imaginary "phenomena." Astrology, numerology, UFOs, alien abductions, Holocaust denial, the face on Mars, "chemtrails," innumerable media-centered conspiracy theories and fluoride-phobia thrive because they inhabit that magical nexus where paranoia meets superstition—fertile ground for fomenting fear.*

The United States Public Health Service estimates that every dollar spent fluoridating water saves fifty dollars in dental expenses. If fluoridation is truly just another conspiracy, then at least this is one that *saves* money.

> "If a court of law held a trial on fluoride's safety and efficacy, the anti-fluoridationists would win."

Fluoridation of Public Drinking Water Is Not Beneficial and Can Be Harmful

Donald W. Miller

In the following viewpoint, Donald W. Miller argues that fluoridation of drinking water is unsafe and ineffective. According to Miller, several decades ago, the officials running the Manhattan Project devised a scheme to make fluoride seem "friendly" because so much of it was produced in the making of the atom bomb. Ever since then, fluoride has been added to public drinking water with the support of the government. Miller says that fluoride is a poison, however, and that ample evidence indicates that fluoridated drinking water causes bone cancer and damages the brain. On the other hand, Miller says that no evidence exists to show that it is safe or effective. Miller recommends completely avoiding fluoridated water. Miller is a cardiac surgeon and professor of surgery at the University of Washington in Seattle.

Donald W. Miller, "Fluoride Follies," LewRockwell.com, July 15, 2005. Reproduced by permission of the publisher and author. www.lewrockwell.com.

As you read, consider the following questions:

1. According to Miller, fluorine is a halogen, like what two other elements?

2. According to Miller, fluoride combines with uranium to form the gas uranium hexafluoride which was used for what purpose in the making of the atomic bomb?

3. According Miller, how many ailments did one researcher say fluoride causes?

Fluoridation of community drinking water began in Grand Rapids, Michigan on January 12, 1945. It was the brainchild of two people who worked for Andrew W. Mellon, founder of the Aluminum Company of America (ALCOA), Drs. H. Trendley Dean and Gerald J. Cox. Mellon was US Treasury Secretary, which made him (at that time, in 1930) head of the Public Health Service (PHS). He had Dean, a researcher at the PHS, study the effects of naturally fluoridated water on teeth. Dean confirmed that fluoride causes mottling (discoloration) of teeth, and he hypothesized that it also prevents cavities. Cox, a researcher at the Mellon Institute in Pittsburgh, was urged to study the effect of fluoride on toothdecay in rats. Determining that it had a beneficial effect, he proposed, in late 1939, that the US should fluoridate its public water supply.

Doctors Did Not Think Fluoride Should Be Put in Drinking Water

Fluorine is a halogen, like chlorine and iodine. It is the smallest and most reactive element in the halogen family (elements with 7 electrons in their outer shell). Fluorine exists in nature attached to other elements as the negatively charged ion fluoride, most notably to hydrogen, calcium, sodium, aluminum, sulfur, and silicon. Sodium fluoride, a by-product of aluminum smelting, initially was used to fluoridate water. Silicofluorides (fluoride combined with silicon), wastes of phosphate fertilizer production, are now used almost exclusively for fluoridation. Fluorine is also present in compounds called organofluorines, where fluorine atoms are tightly bound to carbon. Teflon, Gore-Tex, and many drugs, Prozac, Cipro, and Baycol among them, are organofluorines.

Doctors and public health officials did not think sodium fluoride, used commercially as a rat and bug poison, fungicide, and wood preservative, should be put in public water. The *Journal of the American Dental Association* said (in 1936), "Fluoride at the 1 ppm [part per million] concentration is as toxic as arsenic and lead. . . . There is an increasing volume of evidence of the injurious effects of fluorine, especially the chronic intoxication resulting from the ingestion of minute amounts of fluorine over long periods of time." And the *Journal of the American Medical Association* noted (in its September 18, 1943, issue), "Fluorides are general protoplasmic poisons, changing the permeability of the cell membrane by certain enzymes." But, as Joel Griffiths and Chris Bryson reveal in *Fluoride, Teeth, and the Atomic Bomb*, and Bryson in his book *The Fluoride Deception*, officials in the Manhattan Project persuaded health policy makers and medical and dental leaders, in the interests of national security, to do an about-face and join the fluoridation bandwagon.

Fluoride and the Atom Bomb

Vast amounts of fluoride were required to build the atom bomb. Fluoride combines with uranium to form the gas uranium hexafluoride, which, when passed through a semi permeable membrane, separates bomb-grade, fissionable uranium-235 from the much more abundant and stable uranium-238. This done, fluoride is released into the environment as waste. (During the Cold War millions of tons of fluoride were used in the manufacture of bomb-grade uranium and plutonium for nuclear weapons.) Also, large amounts of fluoride were generated in producing aluminum required for warplanes.

With several instances already on record of fluoride causing damage to crops, livestock, and people downwind from industrial plants, government and industry, lead by officials running the Manhattan Project, sought to put a new, friendlier face on fluoride. This would dampen public concerns over fluoride emissions and help forestall potentially crippling litigation. Instead of being seen as the poison it is, people should view fluoride as a nutrient, which gives smiling children shiny teeth, as epitomized in the jingle that calls fluoride "nature's way to prevent tooth decay."

It worked. Early epidemiological studies showed a 50 to 70 percent reduction in dental cavities in children who drank fluoridated water. These studies, however, were poorly designed. None were blinded, so dentists examining children for caries would know which kind of water they were drinking. Data gathering methods were shoddy. By today's evidence-based medicine standards these studies do not provide reliable evidence that fluoride does indeed prevent cavities.

Based on these studies and its promotion, municipalities across the country started adding fluoride to their water supply. Within 15 years a majority of Americans were washing their clothes, watering their vegetable gardens, bathing with, and drinking fluoridated water.

Still No Proof Fluoride Prevents Cavities or Is Safe

On its 60th anniversary proponents still have not proved that the hypothesis *fluoride [put in public water] prevents cavities and is perfectly safe* is true. The first part of the hypothesis, at least, has biological plausibility. Fluoride prevents cavities by combining with calcium in dental enamel to form fluoroapetite, which increases the resistance of teeth to acid demineral-

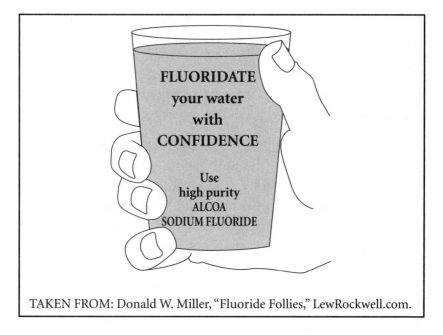

TAKEN FROM: Donald W. Miller, "Fluoride Follies," LewRockwell.com.

ization. And fluoride inactivates bacteria that damage teeth by interfering with their enzymes. But biological plausibility alone is not sufficient to prove efficacy. Epidemiological evidence is required to do that. A debate open to well-informed opponents of fluoridation, if the CDC and ADA [American Dental Association] ever agreed to hold one, would show that existing epidemiological evidence does not prove that fluoride prevents cavities.

In evidence-based medicine, systematic reviews (meta-analyses) are considered to be the best, most "scientific" evidence. A systematic review of water fluoridation studies, published in the *British Medical Journal* in 2000, found, as the chair of the Advisory Group that commissioned the review puts it, "The review did not show water fluoridation to be safe. The quality of the research was too poor to establish with confidence whether or not there are potentially important adverse effects in addition to the high levels of [dental] fluorosis." He adds, "The review team was surprised that in spite of the large number of studies carried out over several decades there is a dearth of reliable evidence with which to inform policy." The case for fluoride does not stand up to careful evidence-based scrutiny.

More Evidence Shows Fluoride Not Safe in Water

Evidence that *"fluoride [put in public water] does not prevent cavities and is not safe"* (the null hypothesis) is more convincing. If a court of law held a trial on fluoride's safety and efficacy, the anti-fluoridationists would win. The judgment in their favor would most likely be beyond a reasonable doubt, or at least on a more likely than not basis. In a courtroom the pro-fluoridationists would not be permitted to employ ad hominem attacks that focus on the character of the opposing witness instead of the evidence, and dogmatic assertions on the safety and efficacy of fluoride would be subject to cross examination.

Proponents of fluoridation will not willingly admit they are wrong. As [author Leo] Tolstoy puts it, "Most men can seldom accept even the simplest and most obvious truth if it would oblige them to admit the falsity of conclusions which they have delighted in explaining to colleagues, have proudly taught to others, and have woven thread by thread into the fabric of their lives."

Changing Their Minds

There are exceptions. Two prominent leaders of the pro-fluoridation movement willingly admitted publicly (in 1997 and 2000) that they were wrong. One was the late John Colquhoun, DDS, Principal Dental Officer for Auckland, New Zealand and chair of that country's Fluoridation Promotion Committee. He reviewed New Zealand's dental statistics in an effort to convince skeptics that fluoridation was beneficial and found that tooth decay rates were the same in fluoridated and nonfluoridated places, which prompted him to re-examine the classic fluoridation studies. He recanted his support for it in "Why I Changed My Mind About Water Fluoridation" (*Perspectives in Biology and Medicine* . . .). The other is Dr. Hardy Limeback, PhD, DDS, Head of Preventive Dentistry at University of Toronto. His reasons are given in "Why I am Now Officially Opposed to Adding Fluoride to Drinking Water." Another former pro-fluoridationist that is fighting fluoride in Canada, and elsewhere, is Richard G. Foulkes, MD, a health care administrator and former assistant professor in the Department of Health Care and Epidemiology at the University of British Columbia. . .

Murray Rothbard (in an article written in 1992) describes water fluoridation as "ALCOA-socialism," arising from "an alliance of three major forces: ideological social democrats, ambitious technocratic bureaucrats, and Big Businessmen seeking privileges from the state." It is a legacy of war, with its call for aluminum and enriched uranium, and the New Deal.

Fluoride Is a Poison

Fluoridation is an especially destructive type of socialism because fluoride is a poison. It is the 13th most common element and one of the most toxic elements in the earth's crust. It is an insidious poison that produces serious multisystem effects on a long-term basis.

Fluoride disrupts enzymes (by altering their hydrogen bonds) and prevents them from doing their job of making proteins, collagen in particular, the structural protein for bone and teeth, ligaments, tendons, and muscles. It damages DNA repair enzymes and inhibits the enzyme acetylcholinesterase in the brain, which is involved in transmitting signals along nerve cells. All cells in the body depend on enzymes. Consequently, fluoride can have widespread deleterious effects in multiple organ systems. One researcher has uncovered 113 ailments that fluoride is said to cause.

The first visible sign of fluoride poisoning is dental fluorosis. It begins as small white specks in the enamel that then turn into spots, become confluent, and, in its most severe stage, turn brown. Dental fluorosis of varying degree affects 20 to 80 percent of children who grow up drinking fluoridated water. Moderate to severe changes, with brown mottling, occurs in 3 percent of children. Dental fluorosis is an indicator of fluoride toxicity in other parts of the body. Like in growing teeth, fluoride accumulates in the brain. One manifestation of "brain fluorosis" in children could be this: Researchers (in China) have found that children living in an area where the water has high fluoride content (4.12 ppm) have IQ scores that are 6 to 12 points lower than children living in a low fluoride district (the difference in IQ scores, at $p < 0.02$, is statistically significant).

Fluoride Has an Affinity for Bones

Fluoride has a particular affinity for calcium and thus for bone; and it poisons bones the same way it does teeth. The average American living in a fluoridated community now ingests 8 mg of fluoride a day. Unlike teeth where the enamel, once formed, remains static, 10 percent of bone tissue is broken down and replaced annually, giving fluoride an opportunity to steadily accumulate year-after-year in bones. People who consume 10–25 mg of fluoride a day over 10 to 20 years, or 2mg/day over 40 years, will develop skeletal fluorosis. The first manifestations of this disease, before there are any changes on x-ray, are joint pains and arthritic symptoms, which are indistinguishable from osteoarthritis and rheumatoid arthritis; muscle weakness; chronic fatigue; and gastrointestinal disorders. In the next stage, osteoporosis develops and bones become more brittle and weak, making them prone to fracture. (The third and final stage, crippling fluorosis, occurs mainly in India where the natural fluoride content of the water is high.)

Soccer Mom Fights Fluoridation

One fall day in 2004, Lea Anne Burke got a call from a neighbor. Had she heard that the city council was talking about adding fluoride to their water supply in Snohomish, WA? For years, the northern end of town had received fluoridated water from the nearby city of Everett. But nonfluoridated water from the Pilchuck River ran through pipes on the south side of Snohomish, where Burke, her husband, and their two little girls live.

Burke, 33, is a soccer mom and vice president of the local PTA. She studied environmental science in college and learned enough about fluoride to be convinced that she didn't want it flowing from the taps in her home. She won't even let her family brush with fluoride toothpaste. So Burke joined a small group of citizens who, last year [2005], persuaded the city council to abandon its plan to fluoridate the water. "Until it's proven safe, why do it?" asks Burke.

If you have only ever known fluoride as a champion cavity fighter that keeps your pearly whites strong, Burke's concerns may sound off the wall. After all, two-thirds of US cities and towns fluoridate water, and most US dentists agree that it prevents tooth decay. In fact, in 1999, the CDC named the fluoridation of community water one of the top 10 public health achievements of the 20th century.

Yet, controversy and doubts about its safety have dogged fluoride ever since the first US city, Grand Rapids, MI, began adding it to its water supply in 1945.

Timothy Gower, "The Danger in Your Water,"
Prevention, June 19, 2006.

There is an epidemic of arthritis, osteoporosis, hip fractures, and chronic fatigue syndrome in the United States. Could fluoride be causing this epidemic? It turns out that even people who live in nonfluoridated areas consume a lot of fluoride, on average 4 mg/day. It is in toothpaste; in fruit juices, soda pop, tea, and processed foods; and, unfortunately, in California wines, whose grapes are sprayed with the pesticide cyrolite (sodium aluminum fluoride). American physicians know little or nothing about skeletal fluorosis, and the early, arthritic stages of this disease mimic other bone and joint diseases. It is a hypothesis worth testing.

Studies show that the rates of bone cancer are substantially higher in fluoridated areas, particularly in boys. Other cancers, of the head and neck, GI tract, pancreas, and lungs, have a 10 percent higher incidence. Fluoride affects the thyroid gland and causes hypothyroidism, which is also an increasingly frequent disorder in the US. Other studies show that high levels of fluoride in drinking water are associated with birth defects and early infant mortality.

Fluoride also damages the brain, both directly and indirectly. Rats given fluoridated water at a dose of 4 ppm develop symptoms resembling attention deficit-hyperactivity disorder. High concentrations of fluoride accumulate in the pineal gland, which produces serotonin and melatonin. Young girls who drink fluoridated water reach puberty six months earlier than those who drink unfluoridated water, which is thought to be a result of reduced melatonin production. People with Alzheimer's disease have high levels of aluminum in their brains. Fluoride combines with aluminum in drinking water and takes it through the blood-brain barrier into the brain. Dr. Russell Blaylock, MD, a neurosurgeon, spells out in chilling detail the danger fluoride poses to one's brain and health in general in his book *Health and Nutrition Secrets That Can Save Your Life.*

Avoid Fluoride and Fluoridated Water

Try to avoid fluoride, in all its guises. It is not an element the body needs or requires, even in trace amounts. There are no known naturally occurring compounds of fluorine in the human body.

Live in a nonfluoridated community. If that is not possible, drink distilled water or tap water passed through a filter that can remove fluoride (a third method using an activated alumina absorbent is not practical because of its expense). Regular activated carbon filters do not work because the diameter of a fluoride anion (0.064 nm) is smaller than the pore size of the filter. It requires a reverse osmosis filter. . . . Distilled water has been given a bad rap by some health writers, which is not deserved. Distillation units are relatively inexpensive.

Fluoride is readily absorbed through the skin (and inhaled). Two-thirds of the fluoride we take into our bodies using fluoridated public water comes from bathing and wearing clothes washed in it. Drinking fluoride-free water in a fluoridated district only reduces fluoride intake by about a third.

One of the greatest public health advances in the 21st century will be removing fluoride from public water supplies.

| "Consumers can trust that bottled water is safe for many reasons."

Bottled Water Is Safe

International Bottled Water Association

In the following viewpoint, the International Bottled Water Association (IBWA) says that bottled water is safe. According to the IBWA, the U.S. Food and Drug Administration (FDA) has strict labeling requirements for bottled water. To be called spring water, purified water, mineral water, sparkling water, or artesian water, bottled water must have certain characteristics. The IBWA asserts that bottled water must meet the same FDA standards that are set for public drinking water supplies. Furthermore, bottled water produced by members of the IBWA, such as Absopure and Fiji, must meet the IBWA Model Code, which in many cases is stricter than FDA regulations. According to the IBWA, the public can be assured that bottled water is safe. The International Bottled Water Association is a bottled water trade group based in the United States.

As you read, consider the following questions:

1. According to the IBWA, bottled water that comes from a well that taps a confined aquifer in which the water level stands at some height above the top of the aquifer can be labeled as what?

2. According to the IBWA, what is the most common technique used to disinfect tap water and which can leave an aftertaste?

3. As described by the IBWA, what is cryptosporidium?

Bottled water is a great beverage choice for hydration and refreshment because of its consistent safety, quality, good taste and convenience. The U.S. Food and Drug Administration (FDA) fully regulates bottled water as a packaged food product and requires bottled water to adhere to FDA's extensive food safety, labeling and inspection requirements. Bottled water is also subject to state regulations and, at the industry level, members of the International Bottled Water Association (IBWA) are required to follow the IBWA Model Code.

Water is classified as "bottled water" or "drinking water" when it meets all applicable federal and state standards, is sealed in a sanitary container and is sold for human consumption. By law, FDA standards for bottled water must be at least as stringent and protective of public health as standards set by the U.S. Environmental Protection Agency (EPA) for public water systems.

Some beverages containing certain ingredients or additives may cause that product to be classified as a soft drink, dietary supplement or some other categorization. Soda water, seltzer water and tonic water are not considered bottled waters. They are regulated differently, may contain sugar and calories and are classified as soft drinks.

Bottled Water Is Labeled According to Specific Government Standards

FDA has established a bottled water Standard of Identity to define the several different types of bottled water based on specific characteristics of the product. Bottled water products meeting the Standard of Identity may be labeled as bottled water or drinking water, or one or more of the following terms:

Spring Water—Bottled water derived from an underground formation from which water flows naturally to the surface of the earth. Spring water must be collected only at the spring or through a borehole tapping the underground formation feeding the spring. . . .

Purified Water—Water that has been produced by distillation, deionization, reverse osmosis or other suitable processes while meeting the definition of purified water in the United States Pharmacopoeia may be labeled as purified bottled water. Other suitable product names for bottled water treated by one of the above processes may include "distilled water" if it is produced by distillation, "deionized water" if it is produced by deionization or "reverse osmosis water" if the process used is reverse osmosis. Alternatively, "_____ drinking water" can be used with the blank being filled in with one of the terms defined in this paragraph (e.g., "purified drinking water" or "distilled drinking water").

Mineral Water—Bottled water containing not less than 250 parts per million total dissolved solids may be labeled as mineral water. Mineral water is distinguished from other types of bottled water by its constant level and relative proportions of mineral and trace elements at the point of emergence from the source. No minerals can be added to this product.

Sparkling Bottled Water—Water that after treatment, and possible replacement with carbon dioxide, contains the same amount of carbon dioxide that it had as it emerged from the

Top Bottled Water Consuming Countries, 2004

Country	Liters Consumed Per Person	Rank	1000 Cubic Meters By Country Total	Rank
Italy	184	1st	10,661	5th
U.S.	91	11th	25,893	1st
Mexico	169	2nd	17,683	2nd
China	9	61st	11,894	3rd
Saudi Arabia	88	12th	2,270	13th
Canada	34.3	37th	1,116	21st

TAKEN FROM: Pacific Institute, http://www.pacinst.org/topics/ water_and_sustainability/bottled_water/. Original source: Peter Gleick, *The World Water: 2006–2007*, Island Press.

source. Sparkling bottled waters may be labeled as "sparkling drinking water," "sparkling mineral water," "sparkling spring water," etc.

Artesian Water/Artesian Well Water—Bottled water from a well that taps a confined aquifer (a water-bearing underground layer of rock or sand) in which the water level stands at some height above the top of the aquifer.

Well Water—Bottled water from a hole bored, drilled or otherwise constructed in the ground, which taps the water aquifer.

Bottled Water Meets Strict Safety Standards

Consumers can trust that bottled water is safe for many reasons. First, bottled water is strictly regulated at the federal level by FDA and at the state level by state agencies. By law, FDA standards for bottled water must be at least as stringent and protective of public health as standards set by EPA for public water systems. This helps ensure that bottled water sold in the United States meets stringent standards for safety, quality and labeling. In addition, members of IBWA must meet strict industry standards required by the IBWA Model Code, which in several cases are stricter than FDA, state or EPA's public drinking water standards. To help ensure that bottled water is as safe and of the highest quality possible, all IBWA members use one or more of the following practices: source protection and monitoring, reverse osmosis, distillation, filtration, ozonation and ultraviolet light.

Bottled water is produced and distributed as a packaged food product and made specifically for drinking. As a packaged food product, bottled water must adhere to FDA Good Manufacturing Practices (GMPs) required of all FDA-regulated food products as well as specific GMPs unique to bottled water production and packaging. GMPs require that each container of bottled water is produced in a sanitary environment and packaged in sanitary, safety sealed containers that are approved by FDA for food contact. Bottled water is also subject to FDA food recall, misbranding and food adulteration provisions, which help ensure that consumers receive safe, high quality bottled water and protects consumers from substandard products.

In addition, members of the IBWA abide by the IBWA Model Code, which includes a voluntary system called HACCP (Hazard Analysis and Critical Control Points). This system was developed by FDA and the U.S. Department of Agriculture (USDA) and adopted by IBWA as a science-based approach to helping ensure safety in every step of the bottled water process.

Taste is another reason consumers choose bottled water. Chlorine is most often used to disinfect tap water and can leave an aftertaste. Some bottlers use ozonation, a form of supercharged oxygen and/or ultraviolet light as the final disinfecting agent, neither of which leaves an aftertaste.

Bottled water provides consumers with consistent safety, high quality, good taste and convenient portability. To help ensure that bottled water is safe and of the highest quality possible, all IBWA members use one or more of the following steps found in a multi-barrier approach: source protection and monitoring, reverse osmosis, distillation, filtration, ozonation and disinfection.

Standards Help Ensure That Bottled Water Does Not Contain Cryptosporidium

Cryptosporidium is a waterborne parasite that lives in animals and can be passed into surface water through their waste. Cryptosporidia from animal waste have been found in rivers, streams, lakes, reservoirs and many other types of surface water. FDA's definition of bottled water from ground water sources [21 CFR §165.110(a)(2)(ii)] states that "ground water must not be under direct influence of surface water," and therefore is not expected to contain Cryptosporidium.

According to FDA bottled water GMPs, bottled water companies are required to use approved sources. There are two types of sources from which bottled water can be drawn: The first consists of natural sources (e.g., springs and artesian wells). By law, these sources must be protected from surface intrusion and other environmental influences. This requirement helps ensure that surface water contaminants such as Cryptosporidium and Giardia are not present. The second source of bottled water consists of approved potable municipal supplies. Bottled water companies that use these sources typically reprocess this water using methods such as distillation, reverse osmosis, ozonation, deionization and filtration. This ensures that the finished product is very different—in composition and taste—from the original source water.

All IBWA member companies that use municipal supplies are required by the IBWA Model Code to employ as a safeguard at least one of three processing methods recommended by the Centers for Disease Control and Prevention for effective removal of microbial (surface water) contaminants, including Cryptosporidium. These processing methods are reverse osmosis, filtration and distillation. Ozonation and ultraviolet light may also be effective treatments for Cryptosporidium inactivation. . . .

You Can Be Assured That Bottled Water Is Safe

The bottled water industry is regulated on three levels: federal, state and, for members of IBWA, at the industry level.

FDA regulations, coupled with state and industry standards, offer consumers assurance that the bottled water they purchase is stringently regulated and tested, and is of the highest quality. IBWA has been a long-standing proponent of sensible regulations for bottled water that help to further ensure safety and protect consumers. IBWA is active at all levels of local, state and federal government, assisting in the development of such regulations, where they help enhance public safety and product quality.

> "Consumer confidence in the purity of
> bottled water is simply not justified."

Bottled Water May
Be Harmful

Olga Naidenko, Nneka Leiba, Renee Sharp, and
Jane Houlihan

*In the following viewpoint, Olga Naidenko, Nneka Leiba, Renee
Sharp, and Jane Houlihan of the Environmental Working Group
(EWG) contend that bottled water may be harmful. According to
the EWG, the bottled water industry charges exorbitant prices
for its water, suggesting that it is safe and pure and much better
than the water coming from the tap. The EWG says that, in reality, bottled water contains chemical pollutants and, in some
cases, even bacteria. The EWG asserts that some brands tested
are probably nothing more than municipal drinking water. The
EWG believes that the standards governing bottled water must
be strengthened. Environmental Working Group is a nonprofit
environmental organization with a mission to use the power of
public information to protect public health and the environment.*

As you read, consider the following questions:

1. According to the Environmental Working Group (EWG), bottled water was purchased from grocery stores and other retailers in how many states?

2. According to the EWG, in addition to disinfection by-products, the bottled water they tested contained what common urban wastewater pollutants?

3. According to the EWG, in conjunction with their testing program, they conducted a survey of 228 brands of bottled water and found that fewer than half describe what?

The bottled water industry promotes an image of purity, but comprehensive testing by the Environmental Working Group (EWG) reveals a surprising array of chemical contaminants in every bottled water brand analyzed, including toxic byproducts of chlorination in Wal-Mart's Sam's Choice and Giant Supermarket's Acadia brands, at levels no different than routinely found in tap water. Several Sam's Choice samples purchased in California exceeded legal limits for bottled water contaminants in that state. Cancer-causing contaminants in bottled water purchased in 5 states (North Carolina, California, Virginia, Delaware and Maryland) and the District of Columbia substantially exceeded the voluntary standards established by the bottled water industry.

Bottled Water Claims Don't Hold Up

Unlike tap water, where consumers are provided with test results every year, the bottled water industry does not disclose the results of any contaminant testing that it conducts. Instead, the industry hides behind the claim that bottled water is held to the same safety standards as tap water. But with promotional campaigns saturated with images of mountain springs, and prices 1,900 times the price of tap water, consumers are clearly led to believe that they are buying a product that has been purified to a level beyond the water that comes out of the garden hose.

To the contrary, our tests strongly indicate that the purity of bottled water cannot be trusted. Given the industry's refusal to make available data to support their claims of superiority, consumer confidence in the purity of bottled water is simply not justified.

Laboratory tests conducted for EWG at one of the country's leading water quality laboratories found that 10 popular brands of bottled water, purchased from grocery stores and other retailers in 9 states and the District of Columbia, contained 38 chemical pollutants altogether, with an average of 8 contaminants in each brand. More than one-third of the chemicals found are not regulated in bottled water. In the Sam's Choice and Acadia brands levels of some chemicals exceeded legal limits in California as well as industry-sponsored voluntary safety standards. Four brands were also contaminated with bacteria.

Wal-Mart and Giant Brands No Different than Tap Water

Two of 10 brands tested, Wal-Mart's and Giant's store brands, bore the chemical signature of standard municipal water treatment—a cocktail of chlorine disinfection byproducts, and for Giant water, even fluoride. In other words, this bottled water was chemically indistinguishable from tap water. The only striking difference: the price tag.

In both brands levels of disinfection byproducts exceeded safety standards established by the state of California and the bottled water industry:

- Wal-Mart's Sam's Choice bottled water purchased at several locations in the San Francisco bay area was polluted with disinfection byproducts called trihalomethanes at levels that exceed the state's legal limit for bottled water. These byproducts are linked to cancer and reproductive problems and form when disinfectants react with residual pollution in the water. Las Vegas tap water was the source for these bottles, according to Wal-Mart representatives.

- Also in Wal-Mart's Sam's Choice brand, lab tests found a cancer-causing chemical called bromodichloromethane at levels that exceed safety standards for cancer-causing chemicals under California's Safe Drinking Water and Toxic Enforcement Act of 1986. EWG is filing suit under this act to ensure that Wal-Mart posts a warning on bottles as required by law: "WARNING: This product contains a chemical known to the State of California to cause cancer."

- These same chemicals also polluted Giant's Acadia brand at levels in excess of California's safety standards, but this brand is sold only in Mid-Atlantic states where California's health-based limits do not apply. Nevertheless, disinfection byproducts in both Acadia and Sam's Choice bottled water exceeded the industry trade association's voluntary safety standards, for samples purchased in Washington DC and 5 states (Delaware, Maryland, Virginia, North Carolina, and California). The bottled water industry boasts that its internal regulations are stricter than the FDA bottled water regulations, but voluntary standards that companies are failing to meet are of little use in protecting public health. . . .

Broad Range of Pollutants Found in 10 Brands

Altogether, the analyses conducted by the University of Iowa Hygienic Laboratory of these 10 brands of bottled water revealed a wide range of pollutants, including not only disinfection byproducts, but also common urban wastewater pollutants like caffeine and pharmaceuticals (Tylenol); heavy metals and minerals including arsenic and radioactive isotopes; fertilizer residue (nitrate and ammonia); and a broad range of other, tentatively identified industrial chemicals used as solvents, plasticizers, viscosity decreasing agents, and propellants.

The identity of most brands in this study are anonymous. This is typical scientific practice for market-basket style testing programs. We consider these results to represent a snapshot of the market during the window of time in which we purchased samples. While our study findings show that consumers can't trust that bottled water is pure or cleaner than tap water, it was not designed to indicate pollutant profiles typical over time for particular brands. Wal-Mart and Giant bottled water brands are named in this study because our first tests and numerous follow-up tests confirmed that these brands contained contaminants at levels that exceeded state standards or voluntary industry guidelines.

The study also included assays for breast cancer cell proliferation, conducted at the University of Missouri. One bottled water brand spurred a 78% increase in the growth of the breast cancer cells compared to the control sample, with 1,200 initial breast cancer cells multiplying to 32,000 in 4 days, versus only 18,000 for the control sample, indicating that chemical contaminants in the bottled water sample stimulated accelerated division of cancer cells. When estrogen-blocking chemicals were added, the effect was inhibited, showing that the cancer-spurring chemicals mimic estrogen, a hormone linked to breast cancer. Though this result is considered a modest effect relative to the potency of some other industrial chemicals in spurring breast cancer cell growth, the sheer volume of bottled water people consume elevates the health significance of the finding. While the specific chemical(s) responsible for this cancer cell proliferation were not identified in this pilot study, ingestion of endocrine-disrupting and cancer-promoting chemicals from plastics is considered to be a potentially important health concern.

With Bottled Water, You Don't Know What You're Getting

Americans drink twice as much bottled water today as they did ten years ago, for an annual total of over nine billion gallons with producer revenues nearing twelve billions. Purity should be included in a price that, at a typical cost of $3.79 per gallon, is 1,900 times the cost of public tap water. But EWG's tests indicate that in some cases the industry may be delivering a beverage little cleaner than tap water, sold at a premium price. The health consequences of exposures to these complex mixtures of contaminants like those found in bottled water have never been studied.

Unlike public water utilities, bottled water companies are not required to notify their customers of the occurrence of contaminants in the water, or, in most states, to tell their customers where the water comes from, how and if it is purified, and if it is merely bottled tap water. Information provided on the U.S. EPA [Environmental Protection Agency] Web site clearly describes the lack of quality assurance for bottled water: "Bottled water is not necessarily safer than your tap water". The Agency further adds following consumer information:

> *Some bottled water is treated more than tap water, while some is treated less or not treated at all. Bottled water costs much more than tap water on a per gallon basis... Consumers who choose to purchase bottled water should carefully read its label to understand what they are buying, whether it is a better taste, or a certain method of treatment.*

In conjunction with this testing program, EWG conducted a survey of 228 brands of bottled water, compiling information from Web sites, labels and other marketing materials. We found that fewer than half describe the water source (i.e., municipal or natural) or provide any information on whether or how the water is treated. In the absence of complete disclosure on the label, consumers are left in the dark, making it difficult for shoppers to know if they are getting what they expect for the price. . . .

Not Good for Environment Either

This study did not focus on the environmental impacts of bottled water, but they are striking and have been well publicized. Of the 36 billion bottles sold in 2006, only a fifth were recycled. The rest ended up in landfills, incinerators, and as trash on land and in streams, rivers, and oceans. Water bottle production in the U.S. uses 1.5 million barrels of oil per every year, according to a U.S. Conference of Mayors' resolution passed in 2007, enough energy to power 250,000 homes or fuel 100,000 cars for a year. As oil prices are continuing to skyrocket, the direct and indirect costs of making and shipping and landfilling the water bottles continue to rise as well.

Extracting water for bottling places a strain on rivers, streams, and community drinking water supplies as well. When the water is not bottled from a municipal supply, companies instead draw it from groundwater supplies, rivers, springs or streams. This "water mining," as it is called, can remove substantial amounts of water that otherwise would have contributed to community water supplies or to the natural flow of streams and rivers.

Eliminate Double Standard

Currently there is a double standard where tap water suppliers provide information to consumers on contaminants, filtration techniques, and source water; bottled water companies do not. This double standard must be eliminated immediately; Bottled water should conform to the same right-to-know standards as tap water.

Bottled Water Is Not a Sin, but It Is a Choice.

Packing bottled water in lunch boxes, grabbing a half-liter from the fridge as we dash out the door, piling up half-finished bottles in the car cup holders—that happens because of a fundamental thoughtlessness. It's only marginally more trouble to have reusable water bottles, cleaned and filled and tucked in the lunch box or the fridge. We just can't be bothered. And in a world in which 1 billion people have no reliable source of drinking water, and 3,000 children a day die from diseases caught from tainted water, that conspicuous consumption of bottled water that we don't need seems wasteful, and perhaps cavalier.

The most common question the U.S. employees of Fiji Water still get is, "Does it really come from Fiji?" We're choosing Fiji Water because of the hibiscus blossom on the beautiful square bottle, we're choosing it because of the silky taste. We're seduced by the *idea* of a bottle of water from Fiji. We just don't believe it really comes from Fiji. What kind of a choice is that?

Once you understand the resources mustered to deliver the bottle of water, it's reasonable to ask as you reach for the next bottle, not just "Does the value to me equal the 99 cents I'm about to spend?" but "Does the value equal the impact I'm about to leave behind?"

Simply asking the question takes the carelessness out of the transaction. And once you understand where the water comes from, and how it got here, it's hard to look at that bottle in the same way again.

Charles Fishman, "Message in a Bottle,"
Fast Company, December 19, 2007. www.fastcompany.com.

To bring bottled water up to the standards of tap water we recommend:

- Full disclosure of all test results for all contaminants. This must be done in a way that is readily available to the public.

- Disclosure of all treatment techniques used to purify the water, and:

- Clear and specific disclosure of the name and location of the source water.

To ensure that public health and the environment are protected, we recommend:

- Federal, state, and local policy makers must strengthen protections for rivers, streams, and groundwater that serve as America's drinking water sources. Even though it is not necessarily any healthier, some Americans turn to bottled water in part because they distrust the quality of their tap water. And sometimes this is for good reason. Some drinking water (tap and bottled) is grossly polluted at its source—in rivers, streams, and underground aquifers fouled by decades of wastes that generations of political and business leaders have dismissed, ignored, and left for others to solve. A 2005 EWG study found nearly 300 contaminants in drinking water all across the country. Source water protection programs must be improved, implemented, and enforced nationwide. The environmental impacts associated with bottled water production and distribution aggravate the nation's water quality problems rather than contributing to their solution.

- Consumers should drink filtered tap water instead of bottled water. Americans pay an average of two-tenths of a cent per gallon to drink water from the tap. A carbon filter at the tap or in a pitcher costs a manageable

$0.31 per gallon (12 times lower than the typical cost of bottled water), and removes many of the contaminants found in public tap water supplies. A whole-house carbon filter strips out chemicals not only from drinking water, but also from water used in the shower, clothes washer and dishwasher where they can volatilize into the air for families to breathe in. For an average four-person household, the cost for this system is about $0.25 per person per day. A single gallon of bottled water costs 15 times this amount.

EWG's study has revealed that bottled water can contain complex mixtures of industrial chemicals never tested for safety, and may be no cleaner than tap water. Given some bottled water company's failure to adhere to the industry's own purity standards, Americans cannot take the quality of bottled water for granted. Indeed, test results like those presented in this study may give many Americans reason enough to reconsider their habit of purchasing bottled water and turn back to the tap.

Periodical Bibliography

Randal C. Archibold   "From Sewage, Added Water for Drinking," *The New York Times*, November 27, 2007. www.nytimes.com.

Marla Cone and Environmental Health News   "Chromium in Drinking Water Causes Cancer," *Scientific American*, February 20, 2009. www.sciam.com.

Daily Times   "25 Million Exposed to Arsenic in Bangladesh: UN," April 6, 2009. www.dailytimes.com.

Jeff Donn, Martha Mendoza, and Justin Pritchard   "An AP Investigation: Pharmaceuticals Found in Drinking Water," Associated Press. http://hosted.ap.org.

Tee L. Guidotti et al.   "Lead in Drinking Water in Washington, DC, 2003–2004: The Public Health Response," *Environmental Health Perspectives*, May 2007. www.ehponline.org.

Kelly Hearn   "Drinking Water Threatened: TVA Tries to Hide Information About Water Contamination from Massive Coal Spill," *The Nation*, April 3, 2009.

Rowan Hooper   "Top 11 Compounds in U.S. Drinking Water," *New Scientist*, January 12, 2009. www.newscientist.com.

Natural Resources Defense Council   "What's on Tap? Grading Drinking Water in U.S. Cities," June 2009. www.nrdc.org.

Science Daily   "What's In Your Water? Disinfectants Create Toxic By-Products in Drinking Water and Swimming Pools," March 30, 2009. www.sciencedaily.com.

Adam Voiland   "Is Your Drinking Water Giving You Diabetes?" *U.S. News & World Report*, August 19, 2008.

Dan Weikel   "O.C. Sewage Will Soon Be Drinking Water," *Los Angeles Times*, January 2, 2008. http://articles.latimes.com.

For Further Discussion

Chapter 1

1. James Hansen contends that sea levels will rise to enormous levels if global warming continues. Nils-Axel Mörner, however, argues that sea level rise and global warming are fictional stories. How does each author view the Intergovernmental Panel on Climate Change (IPCC)? Do they agree in their views about the IPCC?

2. Marc Ribaudo and Robert Johansson from the U.S. Department of Agriculture (USDA) say that agriculture can release many pollutants into surface water and groundwater. The American Farmland Trust (AFT) says that a well-managed agricultural operation can protect and is less detrimental to water quality than developed land. Do you think that Ribaudo and Johansson believe agriculture has benefits? Why or why not? Do you think the AFT would acknowledge that agriculture can release harmful pollutants into water? Why or why not?

3. Andy Buchsbaum contends that invasive species have the Great Lakes on the brink of ecosystem collapse. Alan Burdick, however, asserts that invasive species alone can't destroy an ecosystem. Do you think Buchsbaum has made a strong case in support of his contention? Do you think the Great Lakes might qualify as an exception to Burdick's assertion?

Chapter 2

1. Fred Pearce believes a scarcity of water exists, while Jonathan Chenoweth thinks there is enough water to last for the long term. In their viewpoints, they discuss "vir-

tual water" and the connection between water scarcity and food. Describe how "virtual water" is used to support each author's viewpoint.

2. Alex Stonehill thinks that violent conflicts over water are inevitable, while Andrew Biro doesn't think conflicts will escalate to the level of wars. The authors do agree on some points. What are the things that Biro and Stonehill agree upon?

3. Peter MacLaggan contends that it is time for seawater desalination to play a role in helping to solve water problems. The World Wildlife Fund (WWF), however, is wary of big desalination plants. Do you think MacLaggan's position in the firm Poseidon Resources Corporation might impact his viewpoint, and if so, how? What sorts of things might impact the viewpoint of the WWF? Are your opinions of the merit of each viewpoint changed by your answers to the above questions? Why or why not?

Chapter 3

1. Robert Glennon believes that moving water from agricultural use to urban use is a more efficient use of water, while Tyler McMahon and Matthew Reuer caution that the impacts on rural communities of water transfers could be harmful. Do you think Glennon acknowledges McMahon's and Reuer's concerns in his viewpoint? If so, how?

2. Fredrick Segerfeldt contends that water privatization can save lives, while Wenonah Hauter says that communities are better off without privatization. Both authors use specific examples of privatization that support their contention. Which author's examples do you think are more persuasive and why?

3. Noah D. Hall contends that the Great Lakes Compact is a successful agreement that protects the Great Lakes. Mark S. Squillace says the compact is flawed because it does not

consider existing uses, it is overly complicated, it ignores state authority, and it doesn't adequately protect upper watersheds. Does Hall address any of Squillace's concerns in his viewpoint? How do you think Hall would respond to Squillace's concerns?

Chapter 4

1. Brian Dunning says fluoridated drinking water is safe, while Donald W. Miller says evidence shows that fluoridated drinking water causes cancer. Both authors refer to people who have supported the opposing viewpoint. How do they use their references to these people to support their viewpoints? Who is most effective at doing this? Does it make a difference in your response to each viewpoint that Miller is a doctor and Dunning is not?

2. The International Bottled Water Association asserts that bottled water is safe and must meet rigorous standards. The Environmental Working Group contends that bottled water contains many contaminants and does not have to meet rigorous standards. What evidence do the authors provide for their respective viewpoints, and which author do you think provides the strongest evidence?

Organizations to Contact

The editors have compiled the following list of organizations concerned with the issues debated in this book. The descriptions are derived from materials provided by the organizations. All have publications or information available for interested readers. The list was compiled on the date of publication of the present volume; the information provided here may change. Be aware that many organizations take several weeks or longer to respond to inquiries, so allow as much time as possible.

American Water Resources Association (AWRA)
PO Box 1626, Middleburg, VA   20118
(540) 687-8390 • Fax: (540) 687-8395
e-mail: info@awra.org
Web site: www.awra.org

The American Water Resources Association (AWRA) is a non-profit professional association dedicated to the advancement of men and women in water resources management, research, and education. AWRA provides a common meeting ground for physical, biological, and social scientists, engineers, and other persons concerned with water resources. The AWRA collects, organizes, and disseminates ideas and information in the fields of water resources, science, and technology. The organization publishes the *Journal of the American Water Resources Association*, a monthly journal dedicated to publishing original papers with a broad multidisciplinary approach to water resources issues, and a monthly newsletter, *AWRA Connections*. Five times each year, the AWRA publishes *Water Resources Impact*, a topical and informative journal for AWRA members.

Cato Institute

1000 Massachusetts Avenue NW
Washington, DC   20001-5403
(202) 842-0200 • Fax: (202) 842-3490
e-mail: www.cato.org/contact-form.php
Web site: www.cato.org

The Cato Institute is a libertarian think tank headquartered in Washington, D.C. The Cato Institute supports traditional American principles of limited government, individual liberty, free markets, and peace. The organization's mission is "striving to achieve greater involvement of the intelligent, lay public in questions of (public) policy and the proper role of government." It conducts research on a broad range of public policy issues, holds forums, and sponsors major conferences on public policy debates. The organization is generally skeptical about climate change and promotes water markets. The Cato Institute publishes books, monographs, briefing papers, the quarterly magazine, *Regulation,* and bimonthly newsletter, *Cato Policy Report.*

Clean Water Action

1010 Vermont Avenue NW, Suite 1100
Washington, DC   20005-4918
(202) 895-0420 • Fax: (202) 895-0438
e-mail: mailto:cwa@cleanwater.org
Web site: www.cleanwateraction.org

Clean Water Action is a grassroots organization working to empower people to take action to protect America's waters, build healthy communities, and make democracy work for everyone. Clean Water Action's national campaigns work to impact federal laws and policy, while state offices campaign on local concerns. One of Clean Water Action's primary methods of increasing public awareness are its door-to-door campaigns on issues such as water pollution, global warming, the energy economy, and building healthy communities. Several reports, summaries, fact sheets, and other materials are available on Clean Water Action's Web site.

Environmental Protection Agency (EPA) Office of Water

1200 Pennsylvania Avenue NW, Washington, DC   20460

e-mail: OW-GENERAL@epa.gov

Web site: www.epa.gov/ow

The U.S. Environmental Protection Agency (EPA) is the government agency responsible for protecting the nation's land, water, and air. The EPA enforces the environmental laws of the United States. Within the EPA, the Office of Water works to ensure that drinking water is safe; to protect and restore oceans, watersheds, and other aquatic ecosystems; and to provide healthy habitats for fish and wildlife, plants, and people. The EPA Office of Water issues two electronic newsletters, *Water Headlines*, a weekly online publication that announces publications, policies, and activities of the EPA Office of Water, and *Climate Change and Water*, which offers periodic updates on climate change issues related to EPA's clean water and safe drinking water programs.

Great Lakes Commission

Eisenhower Corporate Park, 2805 South Industrial Highway

Suite 100, Ann Arbor, MI   48104-6791

(734) 971-9135 • Fax: (734) 971-9150

Web site: www.glc.org

The Great Lakes Commission is an interstate compact agency that promotes the orderly, integrated, and comprehensive development, use, and conservation of the water and related natural resources of the Great Lakes Basin and St. Lawrence River. Its members include the eight Great Lakes states with associate member status for the Canadian provinces of Ontario and Québec. The Commission focuses on communication and education, information integration and reporting, facilitation and consensus building, and policy coordination and advocacy. The Commission offers many publications through its Great Lakes Information Clearinghouse.

International Bottled Water Association (IBWA)
1700 Diagonal Road, Suite 650, Alexandria, VA   22314
(703) 683-5213 • Fax: (703) 683-4074
e-mail: ibwainfo@bottledwater.org
Web site: www.bottledwater.org

The International Bottled Water Association (IBWA) is a trade association representing the bottled water industry. The organization seeks to educate the American public about the benefits of bottled water. IBWA publishes several magazines, such as the bimonthly *Bottled Water Reporter*, which covers all aspects of the bottled water industry.

International Panel on Climate Change (IPCC)
Phone: +41-22730820884
e-mail: IPCC-Sec@wmo.int
Web site: www.ipcc.org

The International Panel on Climate Change (IPCC) is a scientific intergovernmental body set up by the World Meteorological Organization (WMO) and by the United Nations Environment Programme (UNEP). The IPCC is composed of scientists from around the world who provide a source of objective scientific information on climate change. The IPCC does not conduct any research, nor does it monitor climate-related data or parameters. Its role is to assess the latest scientific, technical, and socioeconomic literature produced worldwide relevant to understanding the risk of human-induced climate change, its observed and projected impacts, and options for adaptation and mitigation. The IPCC then provides neutral, objective, scientific-based reports to help government leaders make decisions. The IPCC was awarded the 2007 Nobel Peace Prize.

IRC International Water and Sanitation Centre
PO Box 82327, The Hague   2508 EH
   The Netherlands
+31-703044000 • Fax: +31-703044044

e-mail: www.irc.nl/page/5751
Web site: www.irc.nl

The IRC International Water and Sanitation Centre was established by the World Health Organization in 1968 to facilitate the sharing, promotion, and use of knowledge so that governments, professionals, and organizations can better support poor men, women, and children in developing countries to obtain water and sanitation services. The IRC is staffed with internationally recognized specialists and dedicated support staff working in a variety of fields in the water and sanitation sector, including information science, information and communication technology, engineering, sociology, anthropology, economics, and journalism. The IRC Source Water and Sanitation News Service publishes *Source Features and Source Bulletin*, which comes out four times a year, and an electronic newsletter, *Source Weekly*, which is issued 20 times a year.

International Water Association (IWA)
Alliance House, 12 Caxton Street, London   SW1H 0QS
   United Kingdom
+44-2076545500 • Fax: +44-2076545555
e-mail: water@iwahq.org
Web site: www.iwahq.org

The International Water Association (IWA) is a nonprofit trade association representing the water supply and the water quality industries. IWA sponsors conferences and forums on water issues and focuses its activities on water supply to peri-urban, small- and medium-sized cities, and larger towns. It advocates for the provision of sustainable water and sanitation services in developing countries. The IWA publishes several journals, such as the *Journal of Water and Health, Water Intelligence Online*, and *Water Science and Technology*.

Ocean Conservancy
1300 Nineteenth Street NW, 8th Floor
Washington, DC   20036
(800) 519-1541

e-mail: membership@oceanconservancy.org
Web site: www.oceanconservancy.org

The Ocean Conservancy believes that the earth's health depends on the health and vitality of its oceans. The organization seeks to increase public awareness of ocean issues, such as overfishing, off-shore drilling, climate change, ocean trash, and many other issues affecting the oceans. The conservancy wants to significantly change the way oceans are managed. The Ocean Conservancy sponsors the annual International Coastal Cleanup where hundreds of thousands of volunteers around the world pick up trash along the world's oceans and waterways on a single day in September. The Ocean Conservancy issues various special reports such as *A Rising Tide of Ocean Debris and What We Can Do About It* and publishes *Ocean Conservancy* magazine.

The Water Footprint Network
c/o University of Twente, Horst Building
PO Box 217, Enschede   7500 AE
   The Netherlands
+31-534894320 • Fax: +31-534895377
e-mail: info@waterfootprint.org
Web site: www.waterfootprint.org

The mission of the Water Footprint Network is to move the world towards sustainable, fair, and efficient use of fresh water resources by advancing the concept and awareness of the "water footprint," an indicator of how much water is used or consumed by activities or by producing consumer products. The Water Footprint Network develops standards for water footprint accounting and practical tools to support interested people and organizations. The organization facilitates meetings, publications, education, research, and development about the water footprint. Various publications about water footprinting and sustainable use of water are available on the organization's Web site.

Water For People
6666 West Quincy Avenue, Denver, CO   80235
(303) 734-3490 • Fax: (303) 734-3499
e-mail: info@waterforpeople.org
Web site: www.waterforpeople.org

Water For People helps people in developing countries improve their quality of life by supporting the development of locally sustainable drinking water resources, sanitation facilities, and health and hygiene education programs. The organization hopes to see a world where all people have access to safe drinking water and sanitation and a world where no one suffers or dies from a water- or sanitation-related disease. Water For People publishes a quarterly newsletter, *Connections*, various special reports, and a series of audiocasts called *Voices from the Field*.

Bibliography of Books

Peter Annin   *Great Lakes Water Wars*. Washington,
                       DC: Island Press, 2006.

Maude Barlow   *Blue Covenant: The Global Water
                       Crisis and the Coming Battle for the
                       Right to Water*. New York: The New
                       Press, 2009.

Lester R. Brown   *Plan B: Rescuing a Planet Under
                       Stress and a Civilization in Trouble*.
                       New York: Norton, 2003.

Christopher   *The Fluoride Deception*. New York:
Bryson   Seven Stories Press, 2004.

Stephen   *The Lost Language of Plants: The
Harrod Buhner   Ecological Importance of Plant
                       Medicines to Life on Earth*. White
                       River Junction, VT: Chelsea Green
                       Publishing, 2002.

Masaru Emoto   *The Hidden Messages in Water*. Trans.
                       David A. Thayne. New York: Atria,
                       2005.

Robert Jerome   *Water Follies: Groundwater Pumping
Glennon   and the Fate of America's Fresh
                       Waters*. Washington, DC: Island
                       Press, 2002.

Jack M. Hollander   *The Real Environmental Crisis: Why
                       Poverty, Not Affluence, Is the
                       Environment's Number One Enemy*.
                       Berkeley, CA: University of California
                       Press, 2004.

Robert S. Kandel   *Water from Heaven: The Story of Water from the Big Bang to the Rise of Civilization, and Beyond.* New York: Columbia University Press, 2003.

Michael Lannoo   *Malformed Frogs: The Collapse of Aquatic Ecosystems.* Berkeley, CA: University of California Press, 2008.

Bjorn Lomborg   *Global Crises, Global Solutions.* New York: Cambridge University Press, 2004.

William E. Marks   *The Holy Order of Water: Healing the Earth's Waters and Ourselves.* Herndon, VA: SteinerBooks, 2001.

Larry W. Mays   *Water Resources Sustainability.* Columbus, OH: McGraw-Hill Professional, 2007.

Edward McClelland   *The Third Coast: Sailors, Strippers, Fishermen, Folksingers, Long-Haired Ojibway Painters, and God-Save-the-Queen Monarchists of the Great Lakes.* Chicago, IL: Chicago Review Press, 2008.

Robert D. Morris   *The Blue Death: Disease, Disaster and the Water We Drink.* New York: HarperCollins, 2007.

Alice Outwater   *Water: A Natural History.* New York: Basic Books, 1997.

Fred Pearce   *When the Rivers Run Dry.* Boston: Beacon Press, 2006.

Anita Roddick   *Troubled Water: Saints, Sinners, Truth and Lies About the Global Water Crisis*. United Kingdom: Anita Roddick Books, 2004.

Elizabeth Royte   *Bottlemania: How Water Went on Sale and Why We Bought It*. New York: Bloomsbury, 2008.

Vandana Shiva   *Water Wars: Privatization, Pollution, and Profit*. Toronto, Ontario, Canada: Between the Lines, 2002

Richard Joseph Stein   *Water Supply*. New York: H.W. Wilson Co., 2008.

Boyce Thorne-Miller and Sylvia Alice Earle   *The Living Ocean: Understanding and Protecting Marine Biodiversity*. Washington, DC: Island Press, 1999.

Marq de Villiers   *Water: The Fate of Our Most Precious Resource*. New York: Mariner Books, 2001.

Diane Raines Ward   *Water Wars: Drought, Flood, Folly, and the Politics of Thirst*. New York: Riverhead Books, 2002.

World Health Organization and United Nations Children's Fund Joint Monitoring Programme for Water Supply and Sanitation   *Progress on Drinking Water and Sanitation: Special Focus on Sanitation*. New York: UNICEF; Geneva: WHO, 2008.

Index

38⁵⁰

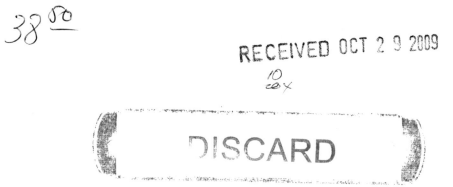